Wholehearted
LOVE

How To Maintain A *Healthy Heart* in *Marriage*

DR. RONALD &
STEPHANIE HAMMOND

Library of Congress Cataloging-in-Publication Data
Hammond, Ronald
Wholehearted Love: How To Maintain A Healthy Heart in Marriage/ by Ronald & Stephanie Hammond

Published in Hamden, Connecticut, by Hope Publishers.

Unless otherwise indicated, scripture quotations are taken from the Holy Bible, New International Version®, NIV®. Copyright © 1973, 1978, 1984, 2011 by Biblica, Inc.™ Used by permission of Zondervan. All rights reserved worldwide. www.zondervan.com. The "NIV" and "New International Version" are trademarks registered in the United States Patent and Trademark Office by Biblica, Inc.™

Wholehearted Love: How to Maintain A Healthy Heart in Marriage
ISBN 978-1-7357184-0-8
© 2019 by Dr. Ronald & Stephanie Hammond
P.O. Box 4028
Hamden, CT 06514

Published by Hope Publishers
P.O. Box 4028
Hamden, CT 06514

Library of Congress Cataloging-in-Publication Data

Hope Publishers

To the loving memory of our powerful, Godly and faithful mother:
Pastor Louvenia Brown
True Foundation Church of God
February 8, 1942 – January 9, 2019

To our Spiritual mother who treated us like her very own:
Annie Mae Roberts
October 12, 1947 – July 26, 2008

To our living mother who we honor because of her
strength and dedication to God and family:
Alma Hammond

WEEKEND

of Love

We invite you and your spouse to attend the Weekend of Love Retreat where you will receive marriage-altering biblical principles that you can apply to your daily lives and make your marriage stronger. In many of our sessions you will learn how to:

- Receive your spouse as a gift.
- Clarify roles as husbands and wives.
- Resolve conflict in the marriage relationship.
- Maintain a vital intimate connection.
- Express forgiveness to one another.
- Create an even deeper level of communication & intimacy.

Our speakers will show you exactly how to pursue a marriage that really works through stories of their own breakthroughs and blunders. We want you to leave the weekend with encouragement, hope and practical tools to build and grow your relationship.

For more details and to register for our upcoming retreats, visit our website at **www.weekendoflove.online.**
If you have questions regarding our upcoming retreats, send us an email at **info@weekendoflove.online.**

Table of Contents

Chapter 1

PROTECTING YOUR HEART

*Guard your heart above all else, for it determines the
course of your life* (Proverbs 4:23 NLT).

If we desire to live peaceably with others, the first thing we must take care
of is our heart. In this chapter we want to draw the parallel between the
condition of our physical heart and our spiritual heart to arrive at some
fundamental truths.

The New Testament uses the Greek
term *kardia* to denote the heart as the center of both physical and spiritual life. In
the physical sense, the heart is the primary
organ and regulator of our blood circula-
tion to all parts of our body. Its pace and
vigor are important indicators of our general well-being.

> The spiritual heart
> is the center and
> seat of all our
> beliefs, attitudes and
> impulses, thoughts,
> passions, desires,
> appetites, affections,
> purposes, endeavors.

The spiritual heart is the center and seat
of all our beliefs, attitudes and impulses,
thoughts, passions, desires, appetites, affections, purposes, endeavors. It is
the seat of our understanding, of our intelligence, of our will and character.
The responses of our spiritual heart are an indicator of our relationship
with God and man.

Let's look a bit further into some important parallels between the physical and spiritual heart.

The Physical Heart

The Sections of the Heart

The human heart comes with four chambers. The first is the right atrium which receives blood and pumps it to the right ventricle. The right ventricle receives blood from the right atrium and sends blood to the lungs to receive oxygen, which then gets pumped into the left atrium and the oxygenated blood is pumped to the left ventricle. The left ventricle, the strongest chamber, then contracts powerfully to pump life-giving blood to the rest of the body. This is what creates blood pressure.

Other vital parts are coronary arteries, which provide blood to the heart muscle, nerve tissues (web) that run through the heart, conducting signals that produce and regulate contractions; then there is the pericardium, which is a sac surrounding the heart for protection.

The heart can be healthy or unhealthy. Since every other system in the body can be affected by the health of the heart, heart health is of primary importance to your physical health and general well-being.

The Spiritual Heart

Like the physical heart, the spiritual heart has four chambers.

1. The Intellect

It has been said that the spiritual heart is, "The thinker in the head, not the thumper in the chest." Quite rightfully so because our spiritual heart:

> The spiritual heart is, "The thinker in the head, not the thumper in the chest."

(a) **thinks**: *For the word of God is alive and active. Sharper than any double-edged sword, it penetrates even to dividing soul and spirit, joints and marrow; it judges the thoughts and attitudes of the heart* (Hebrews 4:12).

(b) **meditates**: *May these words of my mouth and this meditation of my heart be pleasing in your sight, Lord, my Rock and my Redeemer* (Psalm 19:14).

(c) **understands**: *The mind of the intelligent and discerning seeks knowledge and eagerly inquires after it, But the mouth of the [stubborn] fool feeds on foolishness* (Proverbs 15:14 AMP).

(d) **believes**: *"Truly I tell you, if anyone says to this mountain, 'Go, throw yourself into the sea,' and does not doubt in their heart but believes that what they say will happen, it will be done for them"* (Mark 11:23).

Take a moment to evaluate where your thoughts are? Do you meditate on God's Word (Psalm 1:2-3)? Do you have faith? Remember, God looks at your heart, not your outward appearance (1 Samuel 16:7).

2. The Conscience

The spiritual heart can be pierced or cut when it is strongly moved. This is what happened on the day of Pentecost after Peter preached to the multitude who had witnessed the outpouring of the Holy Spirit:

> *When the people heard this, they were **cut to the heart** and said to Peter and the other apostles, "Brothers, what shall we do?"*
>
> *Peter replied, "Repent and be baptized, every one of you, in the name of Jesus Christ for the forgiveness of your sins. And*

you will receive the gift of the Holy Spirit" (Acts 2:37-38, emphasis added).

If our relationships are going to be SAVED (from destruction, infidelity, ungodly ways, addictions), our heart must be soft enough to care about right and wrong and about hurting the God we love. When our conscience is pierced, that should bring us to a place of sorrow. But sorrow is not enough. The Bible makes a distinction between "godly sorrow" and "worldly sorrow;" the first one leads to salvation, and the other to death.

> *Godly sorrow brings repentance that leads to salvation and leaves no regret, but worldly sorrow brings death* (2 Corinthians 7:10).

It is sad that in today's postmodern society, many today do not even blush at sin but revel in their sexual orientations, lifestyles and perversions. Are we outraged at blatant sin the same way the prophet Jeremiah was in his day?

> *Are they ashamed of their detestable conduct? No, they have no shame at all; they do not even know how to blush. So, they will fall among the fallen; they will be brought down when they are punished, says the Lord* (Jeremiah 6:15; 8:12).

When we harden our heart and no longer have the fear of God, the Bible warns us that we put ourselves in trouble. *"Blessed is the one who always trembles before God, but whoever hardens their heart falls into trouble"* (Proverbs 28:14).

Many people have been conditioned by our permissive society to go on sinning because sin is practiced so openly it seems normal. The deceitfulness of the world causes many to go on sinning without any kind of guilt. What is the state of your conscience? Does sin still affect your soul? Does it bother you at all?

3. The Will

The Spiritual Heart:

(a) **purposes**: *But Daniel resolved not to defile himself with the royal food and wine, and he asked the chief official for permission not to defile himself this way* (Daniel 1:8).

(b) **has intentions**: *But the Lord said to Samuel, "Do not consider his appearance or his height, for I have rejected him. The Lord does not look at the things people look at. People look at the outward appearance, but the Lord looks at the heart"* (1 Samuel 16:7).

(c) **obeys**: *But thanks be to God that, though you used to be slaves to sin, you have come to obey from your heart the pattern of teaching that has now claimed your allegiance* (Romans 6:17).

All our external actions originate in the heart (Proverbs 4:23; Jeremiah 11:8). Jesus warned,

"For it is from within, out of a person's heart, that evil thoughts come—sexual immorality, theft, murder, adultery, greed, malice, deceit, lewdness, envy, slander, arrogance and folly. All these evils come from inside and defile a person" (Mark 7:21-23).

> All our external actions originate in the heart.

Let's grant that you intellectually understand God's will, and even believe it in the first chamber. Let's also grant that your conscience is tender enough to be bothered by sin in the second chamber. What about this third chamber? Do you have the will to do His will? Do you desire to do it because you cherish the law of God and hold it in your heart?

Sacrifice and offering you did not desire—
but my ears you have opened -
burnt offerings and sin offerings you did not require.
Then I said, "Here I am, I have come—
it is written about me in the scroll.
I desire to do your will, my God;
your law is within my heart" (Psalm 68:6-8).

4. The Emotions

The Bible also speaks of the heart as having:

(a) **anguish:** *For I wrote you out of great distress and anguish of heart and with many tears, not to grieve you but to let you know the depth of my love for you* (2 Corinthians 2:4).

(b) **desire**s: *Brothers and sisters, my heart's desire and prayer to God for the Israelites is that they may be saved* (Romans 10:1).

> Let our love for God and for others be genuine, from the heart.

(c) **love for God:** *Love the Lord your God with all your heart and with all your soul and with all your mind* (Matthew 22:37).

(d) **love for others**: *Now that you have purified yourselves by obeying the truth so that you have sincere love for each other, love one another **deeply**, from the heart* (1 Peter 1:22, emphasis added).

Let our love for God and for others be genuine, from the heart. As Paul says in Romans 12:9, "*Let love be without dissimulation.*" The word 'dissimulation' (Greek *prospoíisi*) means 'love that is without hypocrisy' – don't let it be fake.

Deep Love

Sacrificial love entails investing your time, resources, emotions, money, plans, and valuables for the betterment of your spouse.

Active Listening. It's about your spouse wanting to listen because they want to hear you talk about your passions, your dreams, hopes, and innermost thoughts. It's about loving you enough to discover who you are and still stay with you regardless of your flaws and imperfections.

Irritating. It's loving in spite of having meaningless arguments about trivia and being able to laugh about it after it's over. You can recognize the mistakes that were made and move on because you mean the world to each other.

Wanting to help. It's caring so much for someone that you want to help them, sometimes more than they want to help themselves and sometimes more than they love themselves.

Jesus said all the commandments could be summed up in two things:

> *"'Love the Lord your God with all your heart and with all your soul and with all your strength and with all your mind';* *and, 'Love your neighbor as yourself'"* (Luke 10:27).

> heart = emotions (feelings); soul = being (life's existence); strength = energy (effort, muscle power); mind = intellect (brain power)

Are you emotionally connected with God and your spouse? Do you truly love Him with all your being? Do you sincerely and deeply love your spouse? How deep is your love for God? Your spouse?

Spiritual Arteries

The spiritual aspect of the heart is the same. We hear countless platitudes about following our heart; but is our heart really a reliable guide? Unless you have first led your heart and filled it with the right inputs, then your heart will be a most unreliable guide. If, on the other hand, you have led your heart and filled it, strengthening it with the right fuel, both physically and spiritually, your heart can be trusted to say and do the right thing.

Looking at the condition of the human heart Jeremiah the prophet laments: *"The heart is deceitful above all things, and desperately sick; who can understand it?"* (Jeremiah 17:9).

> Unless you have first led your heart and filled it with the right inputs, then your heart will be a most unreliable guide.

The Bible has much to say about the spiritual qualities of the heart. Some of it is positive, such as when a person rules his or her heart, and some of it is negative, such as when the heart has been left on its own to absorb whatever the worldly culture is sending to it.

Jesus said that what is in a person's heart shows whether he or she is clean or unclean, and the key indicator of what is inside the heart is what comes out of the mouth (Matthew 15:11-12). What is in the heart will dictate the emotions. For most people, what they feel emotionally will dictate their words and actions.

This is how the heart becomes the leader. The way to lead our own hearts is to decide with our mind and spirit what to put into the heart, how to control the emotions, and how to dictate godly, faithful behavior in obedience to God.

Our heart filters also affect our relationship with the Holy Spirit within us, whose job is to be the Helper in any way we have need of Him, if we allow Him. Is it possible that walking in the love of Christ is seemingly difficult to attain due to an ineffective heart?

Read John 14:16-17 (AMP):

And I will ask the Father, and He will give you another Comforter (Counselor, Helper, Intercessor, Advocate, Strengthener, and Standby), that He may remain with you forever—The Spirit of Truth, Whom the world cannot receive (welcome, take to its heart), because it does not see Him or know and recognize Him. But you know and recognize Him, for He lives with you [constantly] and will be in you.

This same Holy Spirit desires to guide and lead us in the ways we should go; thereby, becoming that filter of what is and is not vital for proper spiritual health.

In the same way when the physical heart has some condition that requires medical intervention, the spiritual heart when affected by some condition requires spiritual intervention.

Heart Blockages

Perhaps you've been to the doctor and were told that you have dangerous blockages to your heart. If your arteries are blocked, then you will have a problem and you will need to get them unblocked with some sort of procedure or a dramatic lifestyle change. We know that a healthy diet is essential to optimum heart health. Conversely, an unhealthy diet contributes to poor heart health which can contribute to heart disease. An unhealthy heart is an over-worked, highly stressed heart, blocked by unwanted plaque lining the walls of the arteries, causing the blockage of life-giving blood flow.

The spiritual heart is no different. Let's say for the sake of imagery that *agape* love is like oxygenated blood. It's all you need to be in a joy-filled marriage (the

> An unhealthy heart is an over-worked, highly stressed heart, blocked by unwanted plaque lining the walls of the arteries, causing the blockage of life-giving blood flow.

Beatles were half right but we don't think they were talking about *agape*). The love gets blocked. What blocks this true love is spiritual plaque. Here are some of the forms spiritual plaque can take:

- Bitterness
- Unforgiveness
- Resentment
- Past trauma
- Unreal notion of love from Hollywood
- Betrayal
- Selfishness
- Mistrust
- Unbelief
- Ignorance of the Bible
- Lies from Satan

All the above issues can cause "heart problems" and must be dealt with. Many of them are connected enough so that if you deal with one blockage, it will take care of another. Bitterness and resentment, for instance, will disappear with the "treatment" of true forgiveness.

> The heart filtration systems void of the work of the Holy Spirit working in and through us lend itself to a recycling of plaque infested thoughts and habits.

The most severe problem on the list is unbelief in the life-changing power of God. Without belief, our worldview will be unbiblical, and the Holy Spirit will be absent. If we face a difficult situation in our marriage, without the Word, we can easily fall into depression or despair. The heart filtration systems void of the work of the Holy Spirit working in and through us lend itself to a recycling of plaque infested thoughts and habits. These thoughts and habits lead our hearts and cause *agape* love to become subordinate to these toxic substances.

Open Heart Surgery

Open heart surgery on the physical heart is used to restore the blood flow, or to replace a diseased heart that has been affected by Coronary Artery Disease, also known as CAD, the narrowing of the coronary arteries (the blood vessels that supply oxygen and nutrients to the heart muscle). CAD is caused by a buildup of

> The spiritual heart requires open heart surgery to unravel the plaque of the past that is trying to obstruct our future.

fatty material or plaque within the walls of the arteries; hence the narrowing of the blood vessels.

The traditional Coronary artery bypass graft surgery (CABG) is the procedure used to treat coronary artery disease. Traditionally, during this procedure the chest cavity is opened and the heart is artificially kept beating during the surgery. The bypass is created from either a vein from the leg or an artery from the chest.

This is an extremely invasive procedure because the blood around the blockage is rerouted so that oxygenated blood can reach the heart through the new graft that has been created.

Similarly, the spiritual heart requires open heart surgery to unravel the plaque of the past that is trying to obstruct our future. What does this plaque consist of? We have mentioned a few above: unforgiveness, bitterness, anger, jealousy and so on. These conditions are considered the works of the flesh, in other words, things our carnal nature likes to express: *"hatred, discord, jealousy, fits of rage, selfish ambition, dissensions, factions"* (Galatians 5:20).

These conditions can clog both our spiritual and physical heart. We have seen how open heart surgery can open the supply of blood to the physical heart, so what can we do with our spiritual heart? The answer is found in the next part of Galatians 5:

But the fruit of the Spirit is love, joy, peace, forbearance, kindness, goodness, faithfulness, gentleness and self-control (Galatians 5:22-23).

No doubt, we can try to love and forgive people with our human spirit and not harbor bitterness or anger. But it is a perpetual struggle because our flesh likes to do as it pleases. But, once we invite the Holy Spirit to take over control, we can move in His power and display His love. It is Christ living in us through the Holy Spirit and no longer our flesh taking control.

> There are strongholds in our mind that we ourselves have created to shield us from attack, the same way scars form around a wound. They have been caused by negative experiences in the past, even trauma, and go back as far as childhood.

There is another solution, too. God has given us weapons that are not carnal but indeed mighty through God to the pulling down of every stronghold. Now the Lord is our fortress and high tower to whom we can run and be safe. But there are strongholds in our mind that we ourselves have created to shield us from attack, the same way scars form around a wound. They have been caused by negative experiences in the past, even trauma, and go back as far as childhood. These are areas in our life that have not been fully surrendered to God. They could be pride, arrogance, rejection, fear, rebellion, deception, lust. All of these have given Satan ground to set up camp in our heart to launch his attacks. But we can pull down these strongholds by repenting and submitting to God's word.

Listen to 2 Corinthians 10:3-5:

We are human, but we don't wage war as humans do. We use God's mighty weapons, not worldly weapons, to knock down the strongholds of human reasoning and to destroy false arguments. We destroy every proud obstacle that keeps people

from knowing God. We capture their rebellious thoughts and
teach them to obey Christ.

How do we do it? By recognizing that such a stronghold exists in our heart, then repenting and asking God to help us overcome. There is no quick-fix solution because, just as these strongholds have been built over time, it will take time to erase the thought patterns and reactions that have almost become second nature to us.

A colleague, who we shall call Amanda, shared with us how her marriage was nearly ruined by her husband's stronghold: rage. This rage was volatile and easily triggered. Sometimes, even over dinner, if she got into an argument with her husband, Mike, and found he couldn't get his point across, he would smash the plates. It got so bad that they had to buy plastic plates. Mike had been a Christian for over 10 years and loved the Lord with all his heart. Though he had somewhat toned down, he still had this deep anger within his heart, and no amount of casting out would make it go away.

Finally, he went through an inner healing program at their local church. With the help of pastoral counseling and guidance from the Holy Spirit, they were able to uncover the roots of the anger. It was a spirit of rejection and abandonment because Mike's parents were both working, and bullying by his two older siblings when he was too small to fight back. The pastoral counseling prescribed was to know the love of the Father through the Word, memorizing key scriptures which related to His acceptance and unconditional love.

Mike was given scriptures to declare and establish his identity in Christ and his own transformation. Want to know some of scriptures that Mike was given to declare?

I forgive my parents and my siblings or any person who has ever hurt me or mistreated me, or caused me to feel rejected or abandoned, in the name of Jesus.

I renounce all hatred, anger, resentment, revenge, retaliation, unforgiveness and bitterness, in the name of Jesus. I put on love, joy, peace, forbearance, kindness, goodness, faithfulness, gentleness and self-control (Galatians 5:20-23).

I renounce all self-pursuit, self rejection, self-hatred, fear.

I am a child of the Most High God and I am accepted in the Beloved (Ephesians 1:6).

I am an heir of God through Christ (Galatians 4:7).

I am fearfully and wonderfully made in Christ (Psalm 139:14).

I am a new creature in Christ, and I have the mind of Christ (2 Corinthians 5:17; 1 Corinthians 2:16).

I am the apple of Your eye; I am hidden under the shadow of Your wings (Psalm 17:8).

I pull down the strongholds of human reasoning and destroy false arguments. I capture my rebellious thoughts and make them obedient to Christ (2 Corinthians 10:5).

I am quick to listen, slow to speak, and slow to anger (James 1:19).

I put away from me all bitterness, and wrath, and anger, and clamor, and evil speaking, with all malice: I am kind to my wife, husband, children and others, tenderhearted, forgiving others, even as God for Christ's sake has forgiven me (Ephesians 4:31-32).

> I pull down the strongholds of human reasoning and destroy false arguments. I capture my rebellious thoughts and make them obedient to Christ (2 Corinthians 10:5).

Mike was taught to stand on Philippians 2:9: "*…At the name of Jesus, every knee should bow…:*" Anger, you have a name but every name must bow to the name of Jesus!

He took the step of addressing this root issue with his parents and siblings, and forgiving them. For a while he also made it a point to avoid controversial subjects like politics.

What happened when the anger would come upon him? He would remind himself that he had self-control. Sometimes he would leave the scene and do something else or he would change the subject. Mostly, he would just laugh. You see, as he started the day praising and worshiping the Lord, he found himself becoming

> Christ was made a curse for us on the cross so that we could be set free from every bondage. Walk in that freedom.

much more joyful and light-hearted. There were times he would give vent to the anger but he was quick to say he was sorry and the episodes became fewer and fewer.

What is your stronghold or strongholds? Yes, it may be anger. But it could be something else: fear and anxiety, depression, jealousy and envy, pride and arrogance, inferiority and timidity, intellectual superiority, sexual sin including pornography, gossip and slander, a critical attitude.

Get help from a relationship coach or counselor and identify the cause so that you cut it off at the root. Christ was made a curse for us on the cross so that we could be set free from every bondage. Walk in that freedom.

Will you pray this prayer with me?

> Father I come to you as Your child, redeemed by the blood of Your Son and made whole by His stripes. Thank You that I am accepted in the Beloved and that no weapon formed against me shall prosper. I bring my heart to You today and confess all my sins to you especially the sin of _____. You know my weaknesses and the struggles I have been going through and I ask for Your

help once again. Help me to walk in total freedom and lead me to the perfect laborers who can help me. I surrender my life to You and I make every thought, imagination, every desire and meditation captive to Christ. I thank You for restoring me completely in Christ. In Jesus' name I pray.

Chapter 2

♥

AN OPEN-HEARTED RELATIONSHIP

So why is it so hard to live out a successful and joy filled marriage? We know the truth, don't we? Shouldn't this be easy? Sin mars everything. Let's turn back now to the heart. Remember that we said earlier that the heart can lead us, or it can be led by us. If it leads us, look out! But if it serves us, then it can be a wonderful ally.

If you are a Christian, then you made your marriage vows on the principle of *agape* (unconditional love) when you committed to love and serve until death do you part. Love is not the issue when a Christian couple is struggling. The love is still there. The issue is that one or both are failing to remember the kind of love, agape, that the marriage is built on. The love is being subordinated to the emotions of the heart. That makes your problem a heart issue.

Agape love in marriage should be the foundational truth which all marital difficulties reference when faced with trials or temptations. When agape isn't the source, then the sinful or fleshly nature becomes the lead, and agape is subordinated.

Going back to the physical parts of the heart, the ventricles and pumps and filters and lungs all serve to keep the body healthy, by keeping the blood healthy and functioning as it was designed by the Creator to be. Just as the heart is extremely important in the processes of physical health, it is extremely important to the processes of spiritual health.

Could it be that walking in the Agape of Christ is seemingly difficult to attain due to an ineffective heart filtration system? Our filters affect our relationship with the Holy Spirit within us, whose job is to be the Helper in any way we have need of Him. We must allow the Holy Spirit to operate as our helper. John 15:26:

> Just as the heart is extremely important in the processes of physical health, it is extremely important to the processes of spiritual health.

> *"But when the Helper (Comforter, Advocate, Intercessor— Counselor, Strengthener, Standby) comes, whom I will send to you from the Father, that is the Spirit of Truth who comes from the Father, He will testify and bear witness about Me."*

The Holy Spirit desires to guide and lead us in the ways we should go; thereby, being that filter of what to allow and what to block out in our proper spiritual health.

Having an Open Heart

To have a successful, joy-filled marriage that glorifies God, we must have an open heart. An open heart trusts the spouse because it trusts God. But do you know that trust is not the most important thing when it comes to relating to your spouse? Do you know that Jesus did not trust everyone? Read John 2:23-24.

> *Now while he was in Jerusalem at the Passover Festival, many people saw the signs he was performing and believed in his name. But Jesus would not entrust himself to them, for he*

knew all people. He did not need any testimony about mankind, for he knew what was in each person.

> When you can allow for weaknesses, because your own identity is firmly rooted in the love of God and His relationship with you, then you can love another perfectly, apart from how they love you.

No, He did not trust everyone the same, but that did not stop Him from loving everyone all the way to the cross. He did not trust His bride to be, but still He loved her and gave Himself up for her. Why is this important? Because people make mistakes. They sin. They hurt us. Do you want your love for people to be based on whether or not they are perfect in how they treat you? If so, avoid marriage at all costs.

But when you can "not trust" and still love, that is the basis of a good marriage. When you can allow for weaknesses, because your own identity is firmly rooted in the love of God and His relationship with you, then you can love another perfectly, apart from how they love you. Isn't that what it says about Christ? While we were enemies with God, He died for us (Romans 5:8). Though He did not trust everyone, He gave Himself for any who would come to Him. He would not turn them away (John 6:37).

> Jesus had an open heart. An open heart says, "I will give you my heart, unguarded even though I know you might break it sometimes."

Jesus had an open heart. An open heart says, "I will give you my heart, unguarded even though I know you might break it sometimes." If we are driven by agape for God and our neighbor, we can risk this possibility, because our heart is protected by trust in God.

A trusting and open heart is built by time and by proof of trustworthiness. It is naïve to trust a person who constantly breaks that trust without repentance or reconciliation. However, starting from a place of love for

God means that someone else's character flaws do not need to hurt our emotions.

Our identity MUST be firmly rooted in Christ.

We get upset and fight when we allow ourselves to be affected by the hurt we receive from others or the lack of approval or rejection when someone shows that to us.

This is a sign of a blocked heart. Truth is blocked. Identity is blocked.

But when we have our identity firmly rooted in Christ and our definition of love is firmly centered on the sacrificial love of God, we can take those hurts in our stride and return love for malice. This, incidentally, is where Jesus is coming from when He expects us to love our enemies (Matthew 5:44). People see the command as demanding and impossible, but He sees it as ultimate freedom because we are resting in His love.

Heart Filters

Imagine if your heart and arteries had no physical filters to clean what is coming into and going out of the heart and going to the body. We need filters for the spiritual aspects of the heart even more. So, what are these filters?

Regeneration

The first filter is the most important, and that is the filter of our rebirth or being born again. Jesus told Nicodemus that he must be born again to see the Kingdom of God (John 3:3). The Holy Spirit must come and regenerate the spirit, or the heart, so that He can make a home in us.

Ezekiel prophesied about God giving us a new heart:

> *"I will give you a new heart and put a new spirit in you; I will remove from you your heart of stone and give you a heart of flesh"* (Ezekiel 36:26).

This happens when we are born again. Our heart that used to be hardened by sin now becomes a heart of flesh, soft and malleable, able to respond to the things of God. Now, we will no longer be slaves to our sin and passions. If you have never put your faith in Jesus Christ for salvation, you must believe that He is the Son of God, that He died on the cross for the forgiveness of your sins. You must call on His name and you will be saved. This is the first step towards gaining a new heart that will serve you instead of leading you.

> Our heart that used to be hardened by sin now becomes a heart of flesh, soft and malleable, able to respond to the things of God.

The Holy Spirit

The next filter, which can be completely inseparable from the first filter of regeneration, is the Holy Spirit. The Holy Spirit lives in us when we receive Jesus into our hearts. His name *Parakletos* means that He walks alongside us. And, because He walks alongside of us, we are admonished to walk by the Spirit and not by the flesh.

> *Those who live according to the flesh have their minds set on what the flesh desires; but those who live in accordance with the Spirit have their minds set on what the Spirit desires. The mind governed by the flesh is death, but the mind governed by the Spirit is life and peace. The mind governed by the flesh is hostile to God; it does not submit to God's law, nor can it do so. Those who are in the realm of the flesh cannot please God* (Romans 8:5-8).

What does it mean to walk by the Spirit? It means to "live according to the Spirit" by setting your mind on "what the Spirit desires." What we think about becomes input to our hearts. It fills our heart. Thinking of

God in Christ, the fruit of the Spirit, the Glory of God, the Love of God, and "whatever is good" (Philippians 4:8), will transform our hearts.

Romans 12:1-2 says,

> *Therefore, I urge you, brothers and sisters, in view of God's mercy, to offer your bodies as a living sacrifice, holy and pleasing to God—this is your true and proper worship. Do not conform to the pattern of this world but be transformed by the renewing of your mind. Then you will be able to test and approve what God's will is—his good, pleasing and perfect will.*

Allow the Holy Spirit to transform you as you renew your mind. Your mind will change as you feed it with good and wholesome thoughts. This is what will change the heart, adding the godly filters so that the heart aids you in your Christian walk, including your Christian marriage.

> Allow the Holy Spirit to transform you as you renew your mind. Your mind will change as you feed it with good and wholesome thoughts.

What do you spend your time thinking about? The truth? The goodness of God? The love of Christ? Or do you think about what the world thinks about – fulfilling your own pleasures and selfish ambitions? The Bible says these thoughts are futile. You will be impacted greatly by your choice in this.

The Word of God

We continuously renew our mind when we read, study, listen to preaching, and meditate on the written Word of God, the Bible. The Bible is inerrant, infallible, and inspired; it is entirely consistent in its teachings. To obey it is to obey God. The Bible tells the story of creation and what went wrong when our first parents sinned. It tells about God's plan to restore the creation to something even better than it was in Eden, by first calling a people for His very own and then sending His Son as the Savior and King of the whole world.

The Word says of itself,

> *All Scripture is God-breathed and is useful for teaching, re-buking, correcting and training in righteousness, so that the servant of God may be thoroughly equipped for every good work* (2 Timothy 3:16-17).

It would be extremely difficult to govern the heart without knowledge and daily attention to the Word of God. Learn to love the Bible. Read it daily. Choose a Bible reading plan and stick to it. Join a Bible study so that you can learn how faithful scholars have interpreted scripture. Meditate on key scriptures. Memorize them. The more you read the Word, the more you will think what God thinks and the more you will develop the mind of Christ (Philippians 2:5). If you find that you struggle to read and pay attention to the Word, it is because we live in a culture that programs us to have a short attention span. Social media and almost all forms of entertainment vie for our attention so that we can do almost nothing that requires focus. But this can be easily undone by a commitment to reading hard things, especially the Bible.

> It would be extremely difficult to govern the heart without knowledge and daily attention to the Word of God.

It is important to be intentional in scheduling time to meditate on the word of God. The desire for God's Word will eventually become as neces-sary as the natural food that nourishes our bodies or the vitamins we take every day. This is what Jesus described in Matthew 4:4 (NLT) when He declared, *"The Scriptures say 'People do not live by bread alone, but by every word that comes from the mouth of God.'"* In the same manner the Word of God, our spiritual food, will begin to sift through our worldly thought patterns and begin to be wholehearted in the things of God.

Come close to God, and God will come close to you. Wash your hands, you sinners; purify your hearts, for your loyalty is divided between God and the world (James 4:8).

The Love of God and Worship

While worship should come first, we list it here because it is the Bible that will tell who the God is that we are to love. Jesus said that the whole law of God is summed up in this one law:

> The Word of God, our spiritual food, will begin to sift through our worldly thought patterns and begin to be wholehearted in the things of God.

"'Love the Lord your God with all your heart and with all your soul and with all your mind.' This is the first and greatest commandment" (Matthew 22:37-38).

The Love of God cannot be separated from Worship. We will talk more in a few moments about God's love, agape, but for now, let's consider how our love for Him is best expressed when we seek to worship Him. If you are a Christian, we hope that you engage weekly with a local expression of Jesus' Church. It is right and good to gather each week with other Christians to worship God corporately and directly, hearing the Word preached, giving offerings, serving one another, and singing together *"in Psalms, hymns, and spiritual songs"* (Ephesians 5:19).

This should be considered the high point of your week because it sets the tone for the whole week. We worship Him together on Sunday, choosing to engage our minds and hearts in the activity. When we worship,

> *...we all, who with unveiled faces contemplate the Lord's glory, are being transformed into his image with ever-increasing glory, which comes from the Lord, who is the Spirit* (2 Corinthians 3:18).

This means that we grow by means of contemplating God together. This should be done as often as possible because it changes us to be like Him. But it should be done, at minimum, once a week when we gather with the church.

Then, we go out from there to worship God in everything else we do, including how we conduct our marriage and family life. "*So, whether you eat or drink or whatever you do, do it all for the glory of God*" (1 Corinthians 10:31). This takes mindfulness. Such mindfulness on God becomes greater and greater the more we spend time worshiping God consciously and wholeheartedly.

Prayer

Prayer is the act of communing with God. It comes naturally because we have a relationship with Him and want to express our love, praise and thanksgiving to Him. We are also called to pray for our families and loved ones, for our nation, for the lost and anything that the Lord

> Prayer is the act of communing with God.

puts on our heart. To pray is to set aside a special time for Him but we should also talk to Him throughout the day. He is approachable because Jesus has made a way for us to come directly before Him.

Hebrews 4:16 exhorts us,

> *Let us then approach God's throne of grace with confidence,*
> *so that we may receive mercy and find grace to help us in our*
> *time of need.*

How amazing that the God of the universe "*who alone is immortal and who lives in unapproachable light, whom no one has seen or can see*" (1 Timothy 6:16) knows us, sees us, and allows us to approach Him!

Psalm 145:18 says, *"The Lord is near to all who call on him, to all who call on him in truth"* and Psalm 17:6 says, *"I call on you, my God, for you will answer me; turn your ear to me and hear my prayer."*

To be in prayer is to be like our Lord. He never missed the opportunity to seek the heart of the Father in all matters. This was the nature of Christ. It says in Luke 6:12, *"One of those days Jesus went out to a mountainside to pray and spent the night praying to God."* Jesus says that we can ask anything in His name and His Father will answer (John 14:14). He says that if we pray with faith, we can see a mountain tossed into the sea (Matthew 21:21). He says that if we pray according to God's will, we will be answered (1 John 5:14).

Prayer keeps us close to the heart of God. Being close to the heart of God will surely transform our hearts to be like His.

Abiding in Christ

Before He went to the cross, Jesus comforted His disciples by saying that, though He was leaving them, they would never be alone. He gave them the key: abide in Him. Abiding in Him would mean that they could always connect with Him and receive His life. They would also be fruitful. How does one abide? Read on:

> Prayer keeps us close to the heart of God. Being close to the heart of God will surely transform our hearts to be like His.

"I am the true vine, and my Father is the gardener. He cuts off every branch in me that bears no fruit, while every branch that does bear fruit, he prunes so that it will be even more fruitful. You are already clean because of the word I have spoken to you. Remain in me, as I also remain in you. No branch can bear fruit by itself; it must remain in the vine. Neither can you bear fruit unless you remain in me.

"I am the vine; you are the branches. If you remain in me and I in you, you will bear much fruit; apart from me you can do nothing. If you do not remain in me, you are like a branch that is thrown away and withers; such branches are picked up, thrown into the fire and burned. If you remain in me and my words remain in you, ask whatever you wish, and it will be done for you. This is to my Father's glory, that you bear much fruit, showing yourselves to be my disciples" (John 15:1-8).

How does one abide? Through the Word dwelling in us, for Jesus is the Word. Jesus chose an organic image of the vine and the branches to illustrate our absolute dependence on Him for our life. If we remain in Him and His word, we will thrive and bear much fruit.

In our flesh we can do nothing. Jesus Himself did nothing apart from the Father. We are called to remain in Christ, to dwell in and with Him. Always. Every second of every day. Is there something you need to do that would require you to leave His presence? Then you know you cannot do it. Abide. Wake up in the morning, and abide with God, in God. Abide all day in thankfulness and awareness of His presence. Abide on your pillow at night as you drift off to sleep. We are made for relationship with and in God through Christ. We are not meant to function apart from Him.

> In our flesh we can do nothing. Jesus Himself did nothing apart from the Father. We are called to remain in Christ, to dwell in and with Him.

Chapter 3

♥

RESTORING THE RHYTHMS
OF THE HEART

He heals the brokenhearted and binds up their wounds [curing their pains and their sorrows] (Psalm 147:3 AMP).

At times the heart can malfunction. Studies in cardiovascular medicine, as seen in the previous chapter, have shown that there can be a blockage of the heart. Poor habits and unhealthy lifestyles can expose the heart to some irregularities. The heart must heal to be whole and the scars that are left after the healing must be erased.

In the same way broken hearts are the result of unattended emotional wounds. The scriptures urge us to guide our heart because it is the seat of life. The Bible also gives a healing procedure. Psalms 147:3 shows that a restoration therapy is initiated where God heals our damaged tissues, dresses them, and binds up the wounds.

Arrhythmias

This is a cardiovascular condition in which the heartbeat becomes irregular. When the electrical impulses which coordinate the heartbeat are not working well, the heart begins to beat faster or slower. This results in arrhythmia, which can be life-threatening. A failing heart can cause irregular heart rhythm. It may result in a cardiac arrest, eventually causing the entire heart system to breakdown completely.

However, when the condition is treated quickly, it can be reversed and brought back to normal. Early diagnosis and treatment would help salvage different parts of the body that rely on blood supply from the heart.

Unhealthy Rhythms of the Heart

The Bible cautions against spiritual arrhythmia. Just like the biological heart, the spiritual heart of man is designed to maintain a healthy rhythm. The rhythm of the heart in this context could be substituted with "yearnings" or "workings" of the heart which should be drawn to the righteousness of God.

> *He walketh uprightly, and worketh righteousness and speaketh the truth in his heart"* (Psalm 15:2 KJV), which speaks of the normal heartbeat for man, which yearns after the righteousness of God.

However, the spiritual heartbeat becomes uneven when it is not after God's righteousness or when the things it yearns for are not in the direction of God. Whenever the heart begins to beat towards unrighteousness, it is a symptom that the rhythm of the heart is altered.

Psalms 1:1 further defines the normal heartbeat:

> *Blessed is the man that walketh not in the counsel of the ungodly, nor standeth in the ways of sinners, nor sitteth in the seat of the scornful* (KJV).

The right heart condition can be maintained by avoiding these dangerous associations: the counsel of the ungodly, the path of sinners and the seat of the scornful.

The Regular Heartbeat

> Our (yearnings) desires are pumped from the heart. The Bible explains the "pumping" of the yearnings as "conception." James gives us a vivid picture of how our evil desires entice us and then when conceived, they give birth to sin and ultimately lead to death

Medically, a normal heart beats between 60-100 times a minute. These impulses cause the atria muscles to contract, which results in the pumping of blood.

In the spiritual parallel, our (yearnings) desires are pumped from the heart. The Bible explains the "pumping" of the yearnings as "conception." James gives us a vivid picture of how our evil desires entice us and then when conceived, they give birth to sin and ultimately lead to death:

> ...but each person is tempted when they are dragged away by their own evil desire and enticed. Then, after desire has conceived, it gives birth to sin; and sin, when it is full-grown, gives birth to death (James 1:14-15).

A healthy heart rhythm is further emphasized in Proverbs 23:19 (KJV): "*Hear thou, my son and be wise, and guide thine heart in the way.*" This passage urges man to ensure that the heart is in good working condition. When we "*guide*" our heart, we control the thoughts that enter our heart that could cause an irregular beat.

Medically, there are a host of causes of irregular heartbeat such as:

- Heart attack
- Injury of heart tissue from a past heart attack/treatment
- Changes in the structure of the heart
- Heart blockage
- Increased blood pressure
- Hyperthyroidism
- Hypothyroidism
- Diabetes
- Apnoeic sleep
- COVID-19 infection

The external or environmental causes of abnormal heart rhythm include smoking, alcohol, caffeine consumption, drug abuse, anxiety, allergies from taking drugs without prescription, and unhealthy habits.

There are also many causes of irregular spiritual heart rhythms. Having an unsaved heart is one, for we have seen that the heart of unregenerate man is desperately wicked and full of evil. Evils can be likened to high cholesterol in the heart. When the heart of man is unsaved, it follows the leading of the devil to indulge in an unhealthy lifestyle leading to death. But, once we are saved, we are *"quickened"* or made alive and saved from death due to sin. Let's look more closely at this scripture:

> *And you hath he* **quickened***, who were dead in trespasses and sins;*

> *Wherein in time past ye walked according to the course of this world, according to the prince of the power of the air, the spirit that now* **worketh** *in the children of disobedience:*

> *Among whom also we all had our conversation in times past in the lusts of our flesh, fulfilling the desires of the flesh and of the mind; and were by nature the children of wrath, even as others (Ephesians 2:2-3 KJV, emphasis added).*

Before God quickened us and made us alive spiritually, we were dead in our sins, motivated by the lusts of the flesh, *"fulfilling the desires of the flesh and of the mind; and were by nature the children of wrath."* The heartbeat of an unsaved human is always after the lust of the flesh, working to fulfill the bidding of the devil. This is a sheer case of a heart beating too fast.

Case Studies: Missing the Beat

In the Old Testament, we see two men who, through following their own heartbeat, got out of step with God's plan. One walked ahead of his master and the other was too slow and missed his calling.

The first was Gehazi, the servant of the prophet Elisha. Gehazi walked ahead of his master, so his heart kept pacing beyond his master's steps. Greed kept his heart racing after the gifts offered by Naaman the Syrian that his master had turned down. Gehazi's heart coveted the gifts, so he ran after Naaman to request them for himself:

> But Gehazi, the servant of Elisha the man of God, said, Behold, my master hath spared Naaman this Syrian, in not receiving at his hands that which he brought; but, as the Lord liveth, I will run after him, and take somewhat of him (2 Kings 5:20 KJV).

> Greed kept his heart racing after the gifts offered by Naaman the Syrian that his master had turned down.

Gehazi was so enticed by his own desires, he could not see the way and fell into the trap that sin had laid out for him. The same leprosy that left Naaman came upon him.

The man who was too slow was Eli who was derelict in his duties and failed to show leadership as the High Priest. It was a time of moral decay when the Word was absent and everyone did according to the dictates of his own heart. Eli's two sons, Hophni and Phinehas, who were appointed priests, abused their position by corruption and acts of fornication with women at the temple. But, rather than discipline his sons, Eli turned a blind eye to their offenses and did nothing in spite of severe warnings from holy men.

Finally, in a battle with the Philistines, the Israelites were defeated, the ark of the covenant was captured and 30,000 Israelites were killed. This included Hophni and Phinehas (see 1 Samuel Chapters 1-4).

The following is the biblical account of what happened when a messenger brought the news to Eli. Eli, now very old and blind, was resting in his chair:

> "Israel has fled before the Philistines, and there has been a great slaughter among the people. Also your two sons, Hophni and Phinehas, are dead; and the ark of God has been captured."

> Then it happened, when he made mention of the ark of God, that Eli fell off the seat backward by the side of the gate; and his neck was broken and he died, for the man was old and heavy (1 Samuel 4:17-18 NKJV).

What killed him? Very likely a massive heart attack due to the shock. This was aggravated by his poor physical and spiritual condition. He was obese, lethargic, blind and lacked the moral fiber to exercise his spiritual authority as a leader.

The Prevention

We can clearly see from the story of Eli that the process of preventing heart arrhythmia requires living a healthy heart lifestyle. This includes eating heart-healthy food and avoiding high cholesterol foods. It is also important to remain physically active and maintain a good weight. Avoidance of smoking is another prevention tip. For a healthy heart, the ear, nose, and throat passages should be clear of smoke and drugs. This includes the need to avoid or drastically reduce the intake of caffeine and alcohol.

In addition, anger and intense stress disrupt the rhythm of the heart. Whenever anyone is angry, their heart beats faster than normal. Such a person needs to get his heart away from the triggering circumstances and gradually let go of the intense emotions. Some persons have to listen to music or read to get their emotions back in place. Most importantly, regular sleeping habits and sufficient rest can restore stability.

Prevent your Spiritual Heart from Unhealthy Rhythms

What does the Word say about preventing an unhealthy heart rhythm? Remember Proverbs 4:23: *"Above all else, guard your heart, for everything you do flows from it."* The key word is *"guard."* Guard the activities of the heart. Do not allow unwanted yearnings to come creeping in and disrupt the rhythm of your heart.

> "Above all else, guard your heart, for everything you do flows from it."

And, just as you keep the heart fit with physical exercise, you need spiritual exercise to build a healthy spiritual life. We must constantly exercise our faith, put it to work, build it up so we can have healthy growth. If spiritual exercises bring growth, what are some of them?

1. Pray often in the spirit and so build ourselves up in our faith (Jude 1:20).
2. Be rooted and built up in God and established in the faith (1 Timothy 4:6; Colossians 1:23, Colossians 2:7).
3. Examine ourselves to see whether we are in the faith and whether we have Christ Jesus in us (2 Corinthians 13:5).
4. Maintain good works, which are good and profitable to us (Titus 3:8).

Maintain sobriety! Sobriety is all about being in a clear state of heart and mind. The Bible stresses that the healthy heart must be sober at all times, without ungodly influences. 1 Timothy 3:2 offers sound advice to any potential leader who wants to grow: "A *bishop* (overseer) *then must be blameless, the husband of one wife, vigilant, sober, of good behaviour, given to hospitality, apt to teach*" (KJV, parenthesis added). To guard against spiritual

> And, just as you keep the heart fit with physical exercise, you need spiritual exercise to build a healthy spiritual life. We must constantly exercise our faith, put it to work, build it up so we can have healthy growth.

illness, the believer must yearn after sobriety and a lifestyle of self control, discipline, temperance and not being addicted to wine (see Titus 2:2, 2:3, 2:4, 2:6, 2:12).

Rather than indulge, the Bible urges, *"And do not get drunk with wine, for that is debauchery; but ever be filled and stimulated with the [Holy] Spirit* (Ephesians 5:18 AMP). In this passage, the Bible recommends one stimulant that helps us maintain a steady heartbeat – the Holy Spirit.

God Restores the Rhythm of the Heart

He heals the brokenhearted and binds up their wounds [curing their pains and their sorrows] (Psalm 147:3 AMP).

> While doctors may only treat, God cures. And, after curing, He restores wholeness such that there is neither scar nor trace of the disease.

God is wonderful. He heals and restores us to wholesomeness. While doctors may only treat, God cures. And, after curing, He restores wholeness such that there is neither scar nor trace of the disease. Naaman the Syrian general who had leprosy was totally restored and his skin became as smooth as a baby after God healed him and granted him a new beginning.

Who then can restore an ailing heart rhythm? Jesus. He is the only doctor that can restore spiritual vitality. To come to God we must approach Him in faith, believing first of all that He exists and second, that He is a Rewarder of all those who diligently seek Him:

> *But without faith it is impossible to please Him, for he who comes to God must believe that He is, and that He is a rewarder of those who diligently seek Him* (Hebrews 11:6 NKJV).

So come to Him trusting Him like a little child. Come to Him confidently and expectantly. The Bible tells us to come boldly to His throne of grace that we may obtain mercy and find grace to help in time of need (Hebrews 4:16).

God's protocol for restoring the rhythm of the heart is to bring us back into fellowship and communion with Him. This is a description of the clinical Intensive Care Unit (ICU). God places the wounded soul under His intensive care to oversee his healing and proper growth. In this place of rest, let Him speak to you and listen for His voice. He will lead you to green pastures beside the still waters; He will restore your soul.

God also gives you His Holy Spirit to comfort you. In the gospel of John, the Holy Spirit is referred to as the "Comforter" in four different verses. As the Holy Spirit brings comfort to us, He sets our heart rhythm back on track and ministers strength, courage, joy and peace.

> As the Holy Spirit brings comfort to us, He sets our heart rhythm back on track and ministers strength, courage, joy and peace.

God's restoration plan is bathed over by His perfect love which casts out our own fears and anxieties (1 John 4:18). His love overlooks every fault, wiping away every self condemnation and receiving us as His sons in Christ (Romans 8:1;

14-17). He calls the broken and wounded to come to Him and be restored (Psalm 147:3). And, as He heals your soul, He also empowers you to minister healing to others so that He may use you to restore the hearts of men to a regular beat (2 Corinthians 1:4). He calls daily to you saying, "*Therefore remove sorrow from your heart, and put away evil from thy flesh*" (Ecclesiastes 11:10 KJV).

To have a heart after God's heart, you must be obedient in small things.

We can all gain valuable insights from looking at the life of David. Such is God's description of David: "*This is a man after My own heart*" (1 Samuel 13:14). God's heart has no irregular beats and functions with perfection. You may be asking, "How can I have a heart after God's heart, like David had?"

When we first meet David in the Bible, he is tending his father's sheep, a job his older brothers looked down on (1 Samuel 16:11). Jesse, David's father didn't even consider David worthy enough to be a potential king when Samuel the Prophet visited their house to anoint the next king of Israel (16:11). But God saw David's faithfulness in the midst of the tasks that his brothers considered meaningless and degrading. David took these tasks seriously and was faithful to complete them with great care. When an animal of prey attacked one of the sheep, David went after the sheep and rescued it from the prey (1 Samuel 17:34-35).

Sometime later in David's life, King Saul heard of David's skill as a musician and arranged for him to visit the palace. As David played his harp out in the fields among the animals, he never imagined that his musical abilities would someday open the door for him to play before King Saul. But, when it did, David served well and faithfully in this new task (1 Samuel 16:14-23).

Then came war with the Philistines. David's older brothers joined Saul on the battlefield. But where was David? Back tending his father's sheep again, and serving as errand boy for his father (1 Samuel 17:14-15). When Jesse wanted David to go find out about his brothers' welfare, he carefully made provision for his shepherding responsibilities and obeyed his father without complaint (17:20).

These seemingly small acts of obedience were big in God's eyes. God chose the shepherd boy to confront the giant Goliath with five pebbles and slay him, that all may recognize the God of Israel and give Him the glory.

Obedience in small things may not seem like much, but it's like the small strands that are woven together to make a rope. The strands which enable us to attack and defeat the marital problems in life are made up of the strands of obedience in the little moral choices that confront us daily: walking in integrity, controlling our thoughts, guarding our hearts, controlling anger, submitting to one another.

Then we are ready to face our Goliaths.

> Obedience in small things may not seem like much, but it's like the small strands that are woven together to make a rope. The strands which enable us to attack and defeat the marital problems in life are made up of the strands of obedience in the little moral choices that confront us daily

Chapter 4

God's Love for His Bride

Before we can move on to how the heart can help or hurt a marriage, we must first talk a little about the love of God for His bride, the Church, out of which springs proper love for our spouses.

For the Christian, how we conduct our marriages is one of the most important aspects of our lives on earth. But did you know that marriage is not eternal? Jesus was asked by some of His critics about a woman who had been widowed seven times with the death of each succeeding spouse; they wanted to know whose wife she would be at the resurrection. He told them that she would be no one's wife in heaven, because there is neither marriage nor the giving of marriage in heaven (Matthew 22:28). But why is this? It is because our eternal spouse is God. We are part of the Bride of Christ. The marriage relationship on earth is only a reflection of our love relationship with God.

Christ and the Church

Marriage, as God instituted it, is intended to reflect the union between Christ and the Church. Paul says so quite explicitly in Ephesians 5, which is one of the most

> Marriage, as God instituted it, is intended to reflect the union between Christ and the Church.

powerful passages on Christian marriage that gives incredible wisdom for married life.

> *Husbands, love your wives, just as Christ loved the church and gave himself up for her to make her holy, cleansing her by the washing with water through the word, and to present her to himself as a radiant church, without stain or wrinkle or any other blemish, but holy and blameless. In this same way, husbands ought to love their wives as their own bodies. He who loves his wife loves himself. After all, no one ever hated their own body, but they feed and care for their body, just as Christ does the church—for we are members of his body. "For this reason a man will leave his father and mother and be united to his wife, and the two will become one flesh." This is a profound mystery—but I am talking about Christ and the church. However, each one of you also must love his wife as he loves himself, and the wife must respect her husband* (Ephesians 5:25-33).

Verse 32 says that the analogy between marital love and the love of Christ for His church is a *"profound mystery"* which we cannot fully fathom in our limited human understanding. It is beyond our imagination but we have Christ's assurance that this is His ultimate purpose for us.

Even in the Old Testament, God would often refer to Israel as His bride. It wasn't just that they were wandering from their Maker when they turned to idols: they were committing adultery towards God. He saw it that way because He saw His faithfulness to her as that of a husband even when she committed adultery by running after other gods.

> *For your Maker is your husband—*
> *the Lord Almighty is his name—*
> *the Holy One of Israel is your Redeemer;*
> *he is called the God of all the earth* (Isaiah 54:5).

How can you say, 'I am not defiled;
I have not run after the Baals'?
See how you behaved in the valley;
consider what you have done.
You are a swift she-camel
running here and there... (Jeremiah 2:23)

As a reflection of God's faithfulness, marriage, too, is meant to be an enduring institution until "death do us part." God is faithful to His bride just as the Church is called to be faithful to her husband. We need to see our marriages in the same way. God brought us together to be a living testimony of His faithfulness to His wife.

> As a reflection of God's faithfulness, marriage, too, is meant to be an enduring institution until "death do us part."

Defining Marriage

Marriage is not a word that needs to be defined, because marriage in and of itself is a definition. When God brings a man and a woman together to be of one flesh, to represent the oneness of the Trinity and to come together to produce offspring, that is called marriage. Theologians refer to this as the conjugal view of marriage.

In the conjugal view is embedded the idea of headship. God is the head of Christ as Christ submitted to the Father. They are equals in every way but with differing roles. Do you see the divine order here? As God is the head, so is Christ the head of the man, and the husband the head of his wife (1 Corinthians 11:3; Ephesians 5:22-33).

This is a profound mystery that our current culture is completely oblivious to. The reason is that somewhere over the last one hundred years the culture shifted its view of marriage from the conjugal view to what is called the revisionist view. Essentially, this view states that rather than marriage being designed by God to glorify Him, to show forth the Trinity, to show forth the love between Christ and the Church, and to produce godly families in the earth, marriage is instead an individual choice for the sake of our personal happiness. When we put our emotional, sexual and personal fulfillment as the primary purpose of our happiness, we may be headed for danger. Happiness in marriage is about turning your attention to God's voice, His provision, and His instruction for your life.

> Happiness in marriage is about turning your attention to God's voice, His provision, and His instruction for your life.

In the revisionist view marriage should, first and foremost, make us happy. If it does not, for whatever reason, then it is all right to discard the relationship. The reason that the Christian divorce rate is essentially the same as the rest of the world is that the Church has fallen for this redefinition. How did this happen? Birth control, which in and of itself is not a bad thing, but it did help to lay the groundwork for this. If marriage is not for having kids, what is it for? Of course, a marriage without kids can glorify God, but removing the aspect of producing godly offspring does move marriage more toward the revisionist view. But more severe was the damage done by the changing of divorce laws in the twentieth century. Wherever there is "no fault divorce," which implies incompatibility, this is the revisionist view of marriage.

Our hope is to show that, if you make marital happiness your goal, you will not achieve it. The revisionist view makes it the goal. But, if you make the love for God, glory to God, and living for God the goal, then you will find marital happiness as a byproduct. So, throw away the unbiblical revisionist view. Lock the door and throw away the key to redefining your marriage. Marriage is, first and foremost, about God, not about you.

> Our hope is to show that, if you make marital happiness your goal, you will not achieve it.

On the other hand, some theologians subscribe to a total permanence view that says under no circumstances can there ever be a divorce and remarriage. That is a massive subject for another time. But, for now, we will follow standard Christian doctrine, which, while subscribing to the conjugal view of marriage, also sees biblical latitude in Jesus' words about divorce being permissible in the case of marital unfaithfulness.

> *"I tell you that anyone who divorces his wife, except for sexual immorality, and marries another woman commits adultery"* (Matthew 19:9).

But even then, we have seen God heal many marriages where adultery was committed, where, through repentance, forgiveness and grace, God restored what was lost.

So, the first thing the heart needs is to be settled on this issue. This will be like the pericardium, which is the protection around the heart. All that follows will not help the one who fails to understand and even love the truth about Christian marriage. Marriage is not for eternity; it reflects the Trinity and points to the ultimate marriage between God and His people, Christ and the Church. Marriage is a defining word, not a word that can be redefined with the times.

One Man & One Woman

And, while we are emphasizing that marriage is a defining word, I would like to establish another key doctrine. Marriage is between a man and a woman and not same-sex couples:

Let's look at Genesis 2:22-24:

> *Then the LORD God made a woman from the rib he had taken out of the man, and he brought her to the man. The man said,*

"This is now bone of my bones
and flesh of my flesh;
she shall be called 'woman,'
for she was taken out of man."

That is why a man leaves his father and mother and is united
to his wife, and they become one flesh.

The union of the man and woman is created by God to be an organic entity. It is not forged by social connections, emotional ties or the will of man, but by God. When a man marries a woman, he leaves his family and becomes "one flesh" with his mate. Though God blesses families as households, He created this "one flesh" union exclusively for marriage.

> Just as man was the only part of creation that was shaped from the earth and "God-breathed" (Genesis 2:7), so also is marriage a distinct work of creation, which differentiates itself from all other relationships.

Just as man was the only part of creation that was shaped from the earth and "God-breathed" (Genesis 2:7), so also is marriage a distinct work of creation, which differentiates itself from all other relationships.

We have established earlier the conjugal view of marriage as part of God's eternal plan: to glorify Him, to demonstrate the love between Christ and the Church, and to produce godly families in the earth. To fulfill such a plan on earth, therefore, the union has to be between a man and a woman. It was never and never will be God's intention for marriage to be between a man and a man or a woman and a woman. To challenge that order to is to challenge the very purpose of that creation, and hence the God of creation.

So we are up against the biblical conjugal marriage versus the revisionist view. "What if marriage could be redefined as "the union of two consenting adults" say the revisionists? And so it is today. Does this supersede God's definition and somehow make same-sex marriages acceptable?

This takes us to the fundamental question: Does God condone homosexuality?

The Old Testament states, *"Do not lie with a man as one lies with a woman; that is detestable"* (Leviticus 18:22; 20:13). This view is upheld in the New Testament, where "homosexual offenders" are among a list of people who *"will not inherit the kingdom of God"*—unless they repent and are cleansed through Christ.

1 Corinthians 6:9-11:

> *Or do you not know that wrongdoers will not inherit the kingdom of God? Do not be deceived: Neither the sexually immoral nor idolaters nor adulterers nor men who have sex with men nor thieves nor the greedy nor drunkards nor slanderers nor swindlers will inherit the kingdom of God. And that is what some of you were. But you were washed, you were sanctified, you were justified in the name of the Lord Jesus Christ and by the Spirit of our God.*

It is God's mercy and grace through the gift of salvation that we can be cleansed from our sin and transformed by the renewing of our mind.

Again, Romans 1:24-26 states:

> *Therefore God gave them over in the sinful desires of their hearts to sexual impurity for the degrading of their bodies with one another. They exchanged the truth about God for a lie, and worshiped and served created things rather than the Creator—who is forever praised. Amen.*
>
> *Because of this, God gave them over to shameful lusts. Even their women exchanged natural sexual relations for unnatural ones.*

In the same way the men also abandoned natural relations with women and were inflamed with lust for one another. Men committed shameful acts with other men, and received in themselves the due penalty for their error.

Was God responsible for their sexual orientation? No, it was because of their unbridled desire for license that God gave them over to their homosexual lusts. In other words, He didn't contend with them anymore; He let them have what they wanted and let their desires take their course. But in due time He would hold them accountable for their error.

The Apostle Peter, too, has this severe warning for homosexual behavior:

...if he condemned the cities of Sodom and Gomorrah by burning them to ashes, and made them an example of what is going to happen to the ungodly;— if this is so, then the Lord knows how to rescue the godly from trials and to hold the unrighteous for punishment on the day of judgment. This is especially true of those who follow the corrupt desire of the flesh... (2 Peter 2:6, 9-10)

We are in the last days and will do well to remember the words of Jesus,

"But as the days of Noah were, so also will the coming of the Son of Man be. For as in the days before the flood, they were eating and drinking, marrying and giving in marriage, until the day that Noah entered the ark, and did not know until the flood came and took them all away, so also will the coming of the Son of Man be" (Matthew 24:37-39 NKJV).

By the time of the Noah, man had become so debased that the whole civilization had to be wiped off the face of the earth, except for Noah's family. Are we in the same time where we can no longer distinguish right from wrong because many of our social laws have normalized sin? Notice that, when the flood came, people were going about their usual activities, even marrying. I wonder whether some of these marriages were same-sex marriages that had become so normal no one even blinked an eye!

> Will the traditions of man replace the commandment of God so we ignore the sanctity of marriage?

My brother and sisters, we have a choice. Will we, like many Christian leaders, choose to be politically correct and condone state-sanctioned same-sex marriages all in the name of being enlightened, tolerant and loving? Let's get a bit closer: will you condone same-sex marriages that are officiated in your own church? Will the traditions of man replace the commandment of God so we ignore the sanctity of marriage?

> *Marriage should be honored by all, and the marriage bed kept pure, for God will judge the adulterer and all the sexually immoral* (Hebrews 13:4).

Chapter 5

♥

TYPES OF LOVE

> Our marriages should be an environment to position our hearts to be totally in it together and to use our hearts in building up our marriages.

We have discussed in Chapter 4 that, for our marriages to be sanctified, we must start with a clear understanding of marriage. We must recognize that our marriages are primarily a means to point to God and glorify Him. Additionally, our marriages should be an environment to position our hearts to be totally in it together and to use our hearts in building up our marriages. We want to talk about the ways to have a "happy" marriage, while remembering that happiness is never the primary goal of marriage. We now realize that making happiness the primary goal is an invitation for Satan to attack our marriage and to attack our hearts.

So let's begin by examining the concept of love.

Agape Love

When most people talk of love they usually are speaking of romantic love. Our culture is obsessed with it. Indeed, most marriages start out under the white-hot flame of romantic love. The Greeks referred to it as *Eros*.

Romantic love is thrilling and pleasurable. Except when it isn't, because the flip side of romantic love is hatred or, worse, indifference. Romantic love is driven by positive feelings, but because of that, such relationships can cause just as much pain as they can pleasure. This is for certain what is behind the 50% divorce rate in the church, as well as the culture at large.

> When most people talk of love they usually are speaking of romantic love. Our culture is obsessed with it.

But God calls us to relate primarily based on something much higher, and potentially much more powerful, even if not as intense emotionally. The Greeks referred to this love as *Agape*. When God existed within Himself and had not yet created anything in heaven or on earth, He was fully satisfied relationally within Himself. God the Father, God the Son, and God the Holy Spirit enjoyed a perfect union, a perfect friendship, a perfect love.

> But God calls us to relate primarily based on something much higher, and potentially much more powerful, even if not as intense emotionally.

It was this love that moved Him to create the universe, and that included creating man in His image. It was this love that caused Him to cover His fallen children in animal skins when they rebelled against Him (Genesis 3:21). It was this love that moved Him to send His only Son to die for our sins, so that we could be forgiven and restored to a love relationship with our Father in heaven, and with one another (1 John 3:11-16).

This is the love that God calls us to when we are commanded to "*Love the Lord your God with all your heart and with all your soul and with all your mind... and love your neighbor as yourself*" (Matthew 22:37-38). And this is the only kind of love with which we could hope to love our enemies and forgive and bless our persecutors. This is the love that binds all our relationships in the church, our brothers and sisters in Christ, and this is the love that binds a husband and his wife. All other love, even romantic love, is deeply subordinate to agape. A marriage that does not subordinate romantic love to the love of the Father will not stand the test of time in a fallen world, ruled by a demon who hates marriage.

> A marriage that does not subordinate romantic love to the love of the Father will not stand the test of time in a fallen world, ruled by a demon who hates marriage.

Eros Love

Extolled in poetry and celebrated in the Song of Solomon, *Eros* love is the physical and sexual intimacy between a husband and a wife. "*Let him kiss me with the kisses of his mouth: for thy love is better than wine*" says the Song of Solomon 1:2.

Within the boundaries of marriage, the Eros kind of love is to be enjoyed, with an intense desire to please your husband or wife. Hebrews: 13:4 says, "*Marriage is honorable among all, and the bed undefiled; but fornicators and adulterers God will judge.*"

It was in this context that God instituted marriage so that we would one day fulfill the calling of pro-creation. Likewise, the love that God has for His people is expressed deliberately in the marital relationship. In the Song of Solomon, there are illustrations of varying intensity and beauty to depict the love relationship between God and those who believe in Him.

By contrast, the world knows this word Eros, purely in terms of "erotica" or "erotic" as in stimulating sexual arousal. The worldly expression has heaped in immediate feelings of arousal, shared between people who are physically attracted to one another. It takes on the mindset much like that of the pleasure principle stemming from pleasure-seeking behavior, immediate gratification, and avoidance of pain.

A marriage based on erotic love will not be long lasting as it is based on the thrills of sexual desire and sensuality, which eventually wane throughout the scenes of life.

Phileo Love

The Greek word *Phileo* denotes brotherly love or the love experienced between close friends. Such love is depicted in acts of generosity and kindness, striving to make the other happy, with no expectations for acts of kindness to be returned.

David and Jonathan are one of the Bible's best examples of *phileo* love within a friendship. In the Old Testament this is conveyed by the Hebrew word *ahab* as in "… *the soul of Jonathan was knit to the soul of David, and Jonathan loved him as his own soul*" (1 Samuel 18:1). Though it was a very deep love, it was brotherly love and not erotic love. Further down the passage we are told all of Israel loved David as a brother – with the same word *ahab* used for love (1 Samuel 18:16).

We find the reference to phileo love in John 21:15-17 after Christ's resurrection. Here Jesus asks Peter if he loves Him three times. The first two times, Jesus uses the word agape for love, but each time Peter responds using the word "phileo" – "*You know I dearly love You.*" This speaks of affection, fondness and liking but falls short of agape love. At the moment this is the place that Peter is at. So the third time, Jesus comes down to Peter's level and asks him if he loves Him using the same word that Peter used – "phileo" (Interlinear bible). God never forces us to agape Him or anyone but will meet us at the level at which we wish to connect.

Love and Headship

> Love is what connects all of us, and agape love is what biblically connects the husband to his wife.

Love is what connects all of us, and agape love is what biblically connects the husband to his wife. The husband is to be the head of his wife (Ephesians 5:23). That means no less than he is to love her, to show her agape. Why is this? Why would God set it up this way? Consider that one of

Christ's roles was to show the Father to His people (John 14:9). Consider that the Jews worshiped *Yahweh*, LORD, although they had never seen Him. Jesus claimed that, since they could see Him, they could see the Father because He was the exact representation of the Father. If they could not recognize Jesus as the Son of God, then they were proving that they didn't truly know the Father, and that Satan was their real father.

But how were they to see God in Christ? We could probably point to several of His characteristics, but the most important way for them to see the Father in His Son is in the way that Jesus loved. This is especially true when one considers the cross. John put it this way in 1 John 3:10-12:

> *This is how we know who the children of God are and who the children of the devil are: Anyone who does not do what is right is not God's child, nor is anyone who does not love their brother and sister. For this is the message you heard from the beginning: We should love one another. Do not be like Cain, who belonged to the evil one and murdered his brother. And why did he murder him? Because his own actions were evil, and his brother's actions were righteous.*

And then in 1 John 3:14-16 it says:

> *We know that we have passed from death to life, because we love each other. Anyone who does not love remains in death. Anyone who hates a brother or sister is a murderer, and you know that no murderer has eternal life residing in him. This is how we know what love is: Jesus Christ laid down his life for us. And we ought to lay down our lives for our brothers and sisters.*

This is astounding. "We know who the children of God are" because they are the ones who love. "We should love one another" because if we do not, we are like Cain, a murderer. This is why we said earlier that the flip side of fake love is hatred.

And then, most importantly, verse 16 says that **we know what love is by the sacrifice that Christ made for us.**

> We know what love is by the sacrifice that Christ made for us.

So, what does this all mean? It means that Christ showed men the Father primarily by modeling the agape love of the Triune God. We know what true love is because we see it displayed in the death of Jesus. Got that?

Now, as Christ is the head of man, the husband is the head of his wife in the very same way, and for the very same purpose, to show the love of Christ, which shows the love of the Father. The husband is to love his wife *"just as Christ loved the church and gave himself up for her"* (Ephesians 5:25), so that his wife can experience the love of the Father through the love of her head, her husband. This is not the love of emotionalist romance novels and movies. This is something much more powerful and enduring. It's a part of a wonderful mystery that the Father invites us to partake of.

> Now, as Christ is the head of man, the husband is the head of his wife in the very same way, and for the very same purpose, to show the love of Christ, which shows the love of the Father.

Chapter 6

♥

THE WHOLEHEARTED MARRIAGE

We've already talked about Christ-centered relationships. We are connected by our commitment to God. We are connected by the love of God without there being any trust. But that doesn't mean that we can't build trust, and that doesn't mean that we can't build connection.

As mentioned earlier, trust is built by time and proof of trustworthiness. It is naïve to trust a person who constantly breaks that trust. We're not saying not to love the person, but to trust an untrustworthy person is foolish and would dishonor God. However, starting from a place of love for God means that someone else's character flaws do not need to hurt your emotions. When Jesus "did not entrust Himself" to men, He could love them despite their weaknesses. When someone hurts you, even if it is on purpose, that is their problem; it's between them and God, their Judge. It does not have to attack your "being," even though it would make sense that you would be sad or hurt.

> With our identity firmly rooted in Christ and having our definition of love firmly established as the sacrificial agape of the Father, we can respond in love no matter how the other side behaves.

No, your identity is firmly rooted in Christ and no one should ever cause you to doubt that. We get upset and fight when we allow our identity to be affected by the hurt or the lack of approval we receive from others. This is a sign of a blocked heart. What is blocked is truth and identity. However, with our identity firmly rooted in Christ and having our definition of love firmly established as the sacrificial agape of the Father, we can respond in love no matter how the other side behaves. This, incidentally, is where Jesus is coming from when He expects us to love our enemies (Matthew 5:44). In some instances our "enemy" can be seen as anyone who opposes us even if they come from our own household, especially when they threaten our peace. People see the command as demanding and impossible, but Jesus sees it as liberating.

So, an open heart is a free heart. Start with Jesus' assumption that no man is trustworthy in their flesh. But also, that your neighbor, even your enemy, and especially your spouse, is worthy of your love, because God is worthy of your love and loving them well is loving God.

Love Connection

You can build connection with others. How? Simply by spending quality time together, getting to know each other, building together. You can build trust in this way as well. While no one is perfect, you should look for those who are the most trustworthy. And, when it comes to marriage, you should endeavor to build trust by first being trustworthy, and secondly, by open and honest dialogue that expects the other to return your trust.

> Connection is closing the distance.

Connection is closing the distance. You love everyone, but you are not close with everyone. That is fine. Your time and energy are finite, and that is what is required to build connection. Your spouse is your number one connection. He or she should get the best of you and your time.

Feeding the Heart & Managing Emotions

Once again, we are saying that the heart is amazing when it is led by us, but it makes a lousy leader. Jesus said, *"Let not your heart be troubled"* (John 14:1). He also said, *"Take heart..."* (John 16:33), implying that we can lead our hearts. And so we can.

We've talked about the most important aspect of leading our own hearts into our service, which is simply a proper understanding of our identity in Christ, and agape love. But there are a few more facts we need to be aware of. You see, when the heart is leading us, it has snuck up from behind and has stealthily taken over. You don't realize it is happening until you are on the brink of doing or saying something foolish, if you have not already done so.

> Satan attacks the heart. Thoughts creep up. You'll notice that the thoughts you "catch yourself" having are not the thoughts you were intending to think.

Satan attacks the heart. Thoughts creep up. You'll notice that the thoughts you "catch yourself" having are not the thoughts you were intending to think. That's Satan speaking his native tongue – lies and accusations – right to the heart. Those lies and accusations start to take root and spread in the heart. You know it has happened when you realize that you are already affected emotionally. At this point most people will do one or both of two things:

1. You will believe the lies and withdraw into your feelings, allowing yourself to feel terrible, self-loathing, angry and resentful toward the other,
2. And you may act on those wrong, deceptive feelings.

But you don't need to do either of those things if you are a person who believes the truth. A person who believes the truth, rehearses the truth and acts on the truth. Satan may try to control your emotions with his lies, but you must train yourself to ignore him. However, before that, you must decide what to input into your heart, rather than letting Satan decide for you. So train your mind to meditate on the right things:

> *Finally, brothers and sisters, whatever is true, whatever is noble, whatever is right, whatever is pure, whatever is lovely, whatever is admirable—if anything is excellent or praiseworthy—think about such things* (Philippians 4:8).

> *You keep him in perfect peace whose mind is stayed on you, because he trusts in you* (Isaiah 26:3 ESV).

You can become a person of "perfect peace" by keeping your mind on the things of God. This can be done in all the ways we've already mentioned: reading the Word, prayer, worship, reading good books, thinking and meditating on the Truth. So, start in a positive direction. Take control over your heart using your mind. Romans 12:2 says,

> You can become a person of "perfect peace" by keeping your mind on the things of God.

> *Do not be conformed to this world, but be transformed by the renewal of your mind, that by testing you may discern what is the will of God, what is good and acceptable and perfect.*

It's so simple that almost no one does it! But commit to this, and your life will change. Your heart will be your ally not only in a great marriage, but a great life!

Although you have attempted to protect your heart with the truth, sometimes Satan will find a way to slip a thought in that you won't notice until your feelings show you there is a problem.

Consider the physical heart. A man or woman may decide to keep it healthy by exercising and eating right. But they may have a blind spot that they don't realize makes them susceptible to some blockage, and they don't find out until there is a problem. Is it too late? Not usually, but lifestyle changes must occur.

> You can become a master of managing your emotions, obeying Christ's command to, "*take heart,*" and "*let not your heart be troubled.*" The more time you give to this, the more quickly you will grow in it.

Similarly, the best of Christians still has this pesky flesh to deal with and still lives all day long in a fallen world dealing with Satan's tactics. Sometimes we get caught off guard, get led into a lie, and our feelings take hold of us, which perpetuates more lies, and more feelings until we are ready to sin. But right here, we can stop it by taking a realistic look at what is going on, root out the lies, and counter them with biblical truth.

In this way, over time, you can become a master of managing your emotions, obeying Christ's command to, "*take heart,*" and "*let not your heart be troubled.*" The more time you give to this, the more quickly you will grow in it.

Care for Your Spouse's Heart

While it is true that you have a hard enough time managing your own heart, remember that you two are now one flesh, so your spouse's heart affects you at a deep level. We will stop short of saying that you are responsible for their heart. You are not. Thinking that you are would lead to destruction. God will not even impose on a person's heart or their will beyond the mysterious process of drawing us into regeneration. But, even in that, He paradoxically leaves our free will intact. No, you are not primarily responsible for anyone but yourself.

But you are responsible to God and to some extent everyone else and, most of all, to your spouse. In this light, we can care for their hearts. But to take full responsibility for their hearts and emotions will destroy you both. He or she may have had a bad day and snap at you, but you will still need to believe the truth about their intentions to only make your relationship better. If you are responsible to him or her, then you can do your part, and continue in joy to trust God. You can speak the truth in love. They must respond. That is their responsibility. But you must keep your responsibilities separate if you're going to have a good relationship.

With that said, what are some ways to care for your spouse's heart?

Some things are gender neutral that each spouse should do for the other. But some things are specific to men's needs and others to women's needs. Here are the things that are neutral:

- Kindness
- Compassion
- Gentleness
- Encouragement
- Help with tasks
- Gifts
- Understanding
- Grace

Here are some things unique to most women:

- To feel attractive and desirable
- To feel loved

Here are some things unique to most men:

- To feel respected
- To feel appreciated

Men and women are very similar in many ways. But the Bible keys in on one aspect in which they are wired differently. This has been written about extensively by Emerson Eggerichs in his book *Love and Respect*. His main thesis comes from the biblical command to both husbands and wives. He notes that, in general, the New Testament authors command husbands to love their wives (Ephesians 5:25). You would assume that it would command wives to love their husbands, but, while it does tell older women to teach younger women to love their husbands (Titus 2:3-5), the direct command to wives concerns respect: that they should respect their husbands (Ephesians 5:33).

If a man wants to build up his wife, he should seek ways to show her love. If a wife wants to build up her husband, she should show him respect. It is not that wives don't appreciate respect, or that husbands don't enjoy love, but, given the choice, most wives want to feel loved, and most men want to feel respected.

Tell a man that you don't respect him, that he is kind of a loser, but that you really love him, and he'll not be your friend. Tell a woman that you respect her, but see nothing lovely about her, and that you just don't love her, and she'll whither. God has designed us differently. If you want to do something that builds up the other, get to understand this principle. Husbands do things that show their wife that she is worthy of their love. Wives do things that show their husband that they respect him for who he is.

Eggerichs also points out that either one can break a cycle of resentment and fighting by choosing to be the first to offer one of these behaviors to their spouse: love to the wives, respect to the husbands. Treating a wife with love will make her more respectful. Treating a man with respect will make him more loving.

Rest for the Exhausted Heart

We know of countless couples who report the same thing: when they are deep into the busyness of life, work, household chores, and raising kids, they have a hard time connecting. Sometimes during busy and exhausting seasons, couples can forget that they like each other, let alone love each other. Sometimes, you can find yourself looking at this person and trying to remember what it was like to just enjoy each other. Those were the good days, but they are so far away in the past. You wonder if you still have the same feelings that you did back then.

> Sometimes during busy and exhausting seasons, couples can forget that they like each other, let alone love each other.

This is the perfect time to get away together. If you are armed with the truth about God and marriage, then you don't necessarily need a regular date night or periodic weekend away in order to keep divorce away; but it sure helps. Why?

Stress is emotionally draining. You use up all your reserves just getting through the day, especially if you have kids, and especially if you have kids plus two full time jobs between you. When you are emotionally drained, then it is harder to face down the lies when they come, to stave off resentments when they grow, to deal with misunderstandings when they happen.

Getting away from all that, especially when it's been tough, is a great way to rest the exhausted heart. You'll have undistracted time to talk, not only about what's been going on, but about other things that are important to you. You'll begin to remember what it was like to have a conversation not about kids or housework. You'll get to know each other in a fresh way and remember why you married each other in the first place.

> Plan a weekend getaway at least once per year. Take at least two nights. The first twenty-four hours is just winding down.

Plan a date at least once a month. If you can't afford childcare, can you find another couple who is willing to trade date nights? One week you can watch their kids, and the next week they can watch yours. Find some way to prioritize this. You'll never regret it.

Plan a weekend getaway at least once per year. Take at least two nights. The first twenty-four hours is just winding down. By the second night, you'll likely feel like a new couple. But a word of caution: if things have been bad lately, this may be where you two make the decision to start relationship coaching or counseling If, after two days you are getting along worse than before you came, then that is because of unresolved issues between you that finally have time to be dealt with. Talk to someone about counseling at church or with a highly recommended marriage coach or counselor.

We are the founders of the Weekend of Love Marriage Retreat (www.weekendoflove.online) an annual marriage retreat whose mission is to equip couples with encouragement, hope, and practical tools to build and grow your marriage. We also strive to arm couples with tools to LOVE each other stronger, LOVE each other better and LOVE in ways that speaks your love languages!

We understand that work, children, activities, running errands and a busy life has a way of overwhelming a marriage. Before you know it, other things are taking priority above the most important thing God placed in your life; your spouse.

The Weekend of Love Marriage Getaway is your chance to make a drastic change. You will experience marriage-altering, biblical principles that you can take home and apply to your daily lives that will make your marriage stronger. Throughout the weekend, through the teachings and couple's projects, you will learn how to receive your spouse as a gift, clarify roles as husbands and wives, resolve conflict in the marriage relationship, maintain a vital intimate connection, express forgiveness to one another and how to create an even deeper level of communication & intimacy.

We conduct both online retreats and in-person retreats as well. For more details, visit our website at www.weekendoflove.online or email us at info@weekendoflove.online.

Heal the Wounded Heart

We have talked already about the wounds we allow to inflict us when the evil one has been working his lies on us. Some of our resentments are because of his wicked interpretation of the past events of our lives. But we have also built up resentments over time because we have been legitimately hurt or betrayed, sometimes by our spouse. We need to face up to these facts.

It can be hard sometimes to know if you have not yet forgiven someone for hurting you. Perhaps you told God, or a friend, or even the person who hurt you that you have forgiven them. But still, whenever the memory of what they did gets triggered, you begin to spiral down emotionally. This is often a sign that there is still some stuff to deal with. Maybe you have not forgiven "from your heart."

Forgive and You Will Be Forgiven

Read Matthew 18:21-22 slowly:

Then Peter came to Jesus and asked, "Lord, how many times shall I forgive my brother or sister who sins against me? Up to seven times?" Jesus answered, "I tell you, not seven times, but seventy-seven times.

Then Jesus told a parable about a servant who was forgiven a great debt and kept out of prison, who then went and refused to forgive a much lesser debt from another servant. When the master found out, he threw him into prison because he did not show the same mercy that he was shown. And then Jesus said,

This is how my heavenly Father will treat each of you unless you forgive your brother or sister from your heart (Matthew 18:35).

The truth is that only those who have received the forgiveness of Jesus Christ for their sins can understand forgiveness. And only those who understand forgiveness can forgive others from the heart. Receiving God's forgiveness for our own sin against Him is a powerful experience. It should change our heart. If you do not feel you can forgive another, you may not have experienced true saving salvation. You either did not believe that God needed to forgive you, or you did not believe that He did forgive you. If this is the state of your heart, go back to Him for His mercy and forgiveness, and then forgive, totally, from the heart. Let God be the judge of those who have hurt you, especially if it is your spouse. Forgive, and you will be forgiven.

> And only those who understand forgiveness can forgive others from the heart.

Fear of the Unexplained

Being triggered emotionally by something could also mean that you need to figure out how that thing was able to happen in the first place, and how you're going to prevent it from happening again. Sometimes we get wounded and our emotions get battered because of fear and confusion. Something about the world doesn't make sense to you. You were hurt because you didn't see it coming. It makes the world, or the marriage, feel like a dangerous and scary place to be in. Betrayal has a particularly powerful effect on our entire world view.

> Betrayal has a particularly powerful effect on our entire world view.

But some processing of it, by journaling or talking it out with someone experienced and mature enough will usually help you to see what you need to see about it. If you try to repress the thoughts every time they come up, you will always be subject to those triggers. Don't repress them. Instead ask God why the incident had to happen. Ask Him if you had any part to play. If your sin was involved, be sure to repent and write down how you will do it differently next time. Ask Him for wisdom to guide you. Determine what you will do if it happens again.

If you were betrayed by your spouse, get your mind clear on the fact that other people's loyalty or fidelity, or the lack thereof, are not the measure of your worth. God's faithfulness is. His creation of you, fearfully and wonderfully in His image is an accurate measure of your worth. It will always be painful to be betrayed or hurt, but a powerful resilience comes from the

> Get your mind clear on the fact that other people's loyalty or fidelity, or the lack thereof, are not the measure of your worth. God's faithfulness is.

combination of trusting God and knowing who you are in Christ. You are not "entrusting yourself" to any human, but giving yourself to those you want to connect with. Knowing what can happen, what it really means versus the lie if something similar occurs will arm you with strength to handle anything through the truth and the power of the Holy Spirit.

All marriages are entered into via a contract – wedding vows that are either verbal or written, stipulating the partners and terms of the relationship. Generally, a husband and wife commit to be faithful to each other and no one else until death. The vows outline the emotional and sexual needs that are expected to be fulfilled in the marriage, and to what extent those needs are exclusive to the partners. Infidelity and betrayal are a breach of contract of exclusivity that you have with your husband or wife. This is considered outsourcing your emotional and sexual needs to others outside the relationship without the consent of your spouse.

Case Study: A Bait

Several years ago, we met Stephen and Jeanette who had been married for approximately 15 years and had children. Their marriage had drifted into something that made Jeanette unhappy. Jeanette's spiritual heart cavity had become hardened from years of unforgiveness that she allowed to affect the spiritual arteries of her heart, which caused blockage of life-giving nutrients to her relationship. Jeannette experienced spiritual heart irregularities that went unattended for some time. This left emotional scars that exposed areas of vulnerabilities. Their connection seemed completely gone. There appeared to be no hope for this marriage. It was evident that Jeanette had not employed Philippians 4:8 over her thoughts to think on those things which were lovely, honorable, true, worthy of respect, pure and wholesome to bring about the peace that her heart was deficient of. The result of not thinking of those things produced unforgiveness.

Then Jeanette met a male co-worker at the office, and they started flirting. This turned into an intense emotional affair that lasted about two months. She thought that she was deeply in love with him and decided that she should really divorce the husband and leave the family since she was so unhappy.

The couple eventually decided to try and work out their marriage, go into couples counseling, and started being intentional about their affection and intimacy. Although it was painful for Stephen, he showed great resilience that came from the combination of him trusting God and knowing his identity in Christ.

Today this couple is flourishing in their marriage. They have raised wonderful children together and are in a better place spiritually and emotionally.

Chapter 7

PATHS TO INTIMACY AND GROWTH

Intimacy

Intimacy is a keystone in romantic relationships. Sexual intimacy is important. Physical closeness and vulnerability can bring couples closer together. Humans are sexual beings. A significant other can provide not only physical and emotional fulfillment but also feelings of safety in sexuality. This safety paves the way for a deeper connection that resonates through the rest of the relationship.

However, intimate relationships are not solely comprised of sexual intimacy. Physical intimacy occurs in friendships with friendly hugs and kisses on the cheek. An active sex life isn't a requirement for a strong and healthy relationship. In fact, there are four other types of intimacy I can think of that are equally important.

Physical Intimacy

Go on a walk while holding hands. Be mindful on a walk together. Hold hands and feel your partner's hand in yours. Notice the comforting feeling this connection brings.

Hug for 30-60 seconds. After the first 20 seconds of a hug, your brain starts secreting a feel-good brain chemical called serotonin. This produces feelings of connection and love.

Give each other a massage. Set the timer for five minutes and give your significant other a small shoulder massage. This will help you connect physically in an intimate way that is also being of service to your spouse.

Cuddle on the couch. Put on a movie and find your favorite spot on the couch. Cozy up together, even if just your legs are touching.

Emotional Intimacy

A secure relationship is one where both parties feel accepted. A great way to participate in a secure relationship is by being emotionally available for each other.

You can express your emotional availability both verbally and non-verbally. Sitting close and making eye contact will also increase emotional intimacy. Listening closely, validating, and summarizing what your partner is saying will show your partner that you are there and willing to listen. It's easy to become emotionally unavailable because it takes such a conscious effort to be available. It requires giving our attention on purpose.

> A secure relationship is one where both parties feel accepted. A great way to participate in a secure relationship is by being emotionally available for each other.

In order to promote more emotional intimacy, there are a few things you can do that will benefit the whole relationship. It all starts with you.

Begin by identifying your emotions. When you can identify what you're feeling, you are better able to communicate and share those feelings. Once you're able to identify your emotions, you'll have a better sense of your emotional needs. What do you need in order to feel fulfilled in your daily life and in your relationship? How can your partner help? The ability to vocalize these needs takes practice, but the results are worth the effort.

Intellectual Intimacy

Heart-to-heart, brain-to-brain. The foundation of intellectual intimacy is all in your head – it's all about how you think and communicate. Being intellectually intimate means sharing ideas and connecting on a higher plane than day-to-day conversations about other people or material things. Intellectually intimate conversations are about the things that really make you think.

> In order to promote more emotional intimacy, there are a few things you can do that will benefit the whole relationship. It all starts with you.

What is the purpose of your life? What are the deepest life lessons you've learned? Having these deeper conversations allows for the growth of intellectual intimacy.

Conversations that we avoid with the whole family at Thanksgiving might be the conversations we have every day at home with our partner. The safety that a healthy relationship provides allows a haven for the growth and development of opinions, ideas, and dreams.

> The safety that a healthy relationship provides allows a haven for the growth and development of opinions, ideas, and dreams.

There is so much currently to talk about: from world events and local politics to new ways of doing business, to things that are on your mind. Be comfortable with each other, listening, asking for opinion, learning from each other and feeling free to share your views.

Grow Together, Not Apart

Each time we experience something new, we grow, even if just a little. Every interaction and every try at something new develops us into the people we will be tomorrow. When a relationship has enough room for both of you to grow, it is more likely to invite positive growth.

A secure and healthy relationship allows time and space to explore and learn new things together. Being in a relationship does not mean you are tied down. In fact, it means that now you have a person to explore new things with. Your life does not get boring as soon as you get married. In fact, that may be when it gets most exciting!

> Your life does not get boring as soon as you get married. In fact, that may be when it gets most exciting!

Always Stay Dating

Comfortability in a relationship is wonderful and necessary. However, too much comfortability may stand in the way of taking new risks and learning new things. You are comfortable together, at home on the couch. So why move?

While every person and every couple needs time to unwind and relax, equally important is the need to get out and try new things together. By going to new events, spending a day volunteering, or trying out a new dish, you're getting to know your partner in new ways.

> While every person and every couple needs time to unwind and relax, equally important is the need to get out and try new things together.

A night at home on the couch is a welcome relief in the middle of a busy month. But be careful not to spend every free moment in this fashion. While it's nice to have someone to lounge around with, it is also nice to spend time in a way that will develop your relationship in a meaningful way.

The fact that you're in a committed relationship doesn't mean that you're no longer dating your partner. Instead, you can keep the flame of newness alive by partaking in fun, adventurous, and romantic outings.

> If every experience fosters individual growth, the new experiences you have as a couple will contribute to the positive growth of your relationship.

You can do this by planning to have a date regularly. This date night is reserved for a new experience. Instead of going to the same restaurant every time, try a new restaurant with food neither of you have had. Or, go to a new destination that you've always wanted to check out.

If every experience fosters individual growth, the new experiences you have as a couple will contribute to the positive growth of your relationship. When you learn something new together, you're strengthening the bond of your relationship and getting to know your partner even better.

A date doesn't need to be expensive or fancy in order to be exciting and inspiring.

Simple Date Ideas

Go to a new outdoor location for a walk. Getting outside and being mindful in nature together will offer an opportunity for each of you to connect in peace.

Try a new type of food. Take time to get ready, the way you did during your first few dates together. Keep the phones away and keep your attention on each other.

Make art together. Sign up for a painting class or go decorate ceramic pottery together. You could even get some craft supplies and have a date at home. Whether you like glitter, hot glue, or woodworking, getting creative together will open the creative potential of your relationship.

Learn something new. Check your local community calendar or online events for any interesting talks you're interested in, such as authors, experts or motivational speakers. Choose a topic you each find interesting and see what there is to learn about it. Afterwards, discuss the event and learn something new about each other.

Serve in ministry together. Take time to volunteer at church where you both can serve together. Perhaps you've always been interested in serving the homeless or visiting the sick. This will provide more than physical growth – it will promote the spiritual growth of your relationship.

Do spontaneous things together. On a quiet rainy day, dump out the 5,000-piece puzzle and get to work. Focusing on this activity, with intermittent conversation, builds experiential intimacy.

The experiences that don't require talking really highlight the quality of the experience. However, experiential intimacy is increased with each new experience you face together, whether you're having conversations about it or not. Doing new things invites new types of conversations, new people, and new memories. These activities will help your relationship grow stronger roots as you weather the storms of life.

Share Each Other's Interests

One way you can grow together is by supporting each other in the things you are each passionate about. Whether the passion is singing or volunteering, dedicate a few hours to letting your partner take the wheel. Encourage them when they talk about it.

When we first got married, I was not a music person at all. Watching my wife over the years and seeing her passion for music and singing has opened me up to her passion. I have

Spend time asking questions, observing and learning from your significant other. Giving this specific attention shows your spouse that you're committed and supportive.

found myself listening to genres of music and artists that I know I would never have been exposed to without her passion and love for music. Early on, I found myself asking her questions about certain artists, songs and music categories because I was simply unaware. Today, we listen to music together and music has brought us closer together.

Spend time asking questions, observing and learning from your significant other. Giving this specific attention shows your spouse that you're committed and supportive.

Relationship Coaching or Counseling

As discussed in Chapter 5, committing to relationship coaching or counseling can be an asset to your marriage especially in times of need. Couples counseling or coaching is a unique opportunity to understand how a relationship works and doesn't work. You don't have to wait for a struggle to work with a counselor or coach. In fact, if you're not struggling, now is a great time to start with a professional.

> Couples counseling or coaching is a unique opportunity to understand how a relationship works and doesn't work.

If both of you are willing, participating together will provide a system of accountability in your relationship. Attending a professional session as little as once per month will ensure that nothing falls through the cracks. Big problems typically begin as small problems. These small obstacles can be discussed before it erupts into a major crisis.

It can be difficult to see the big picture when you're one of the main subjects of the picture. That's why a professional can provide a perspective that is non-judgmental and well-informed. In a healing space, you can learn to enjoy the good and work through the negative.

Continuing to keep in touch with your counselor or coach before a crisis will make it much easier to reach out when a crisis does occur. Work done together in these sessions will give you an opportunity to learn how to be in relationship with one another and it will have a direct effect on the growth of your relationship.

We are Certified Relationship Coaches who have coached many couples over the years. If your relationship needs assistance, please feel free to reach out to us for relationship coaching. We may be contacted at info@ weekendoflove.online.

Chapter 8

RULES OF ENGAGEMENT

> Healthy relationships are beautiful when we can address issues that block our hearts from having a healthy flow.

As discussed in Chapter 2, healthy relationships are beautiful when we can address issues that block our hearts from having a healthy flow. Healthy relationships also experience times of struggle. Healthy people can disagree and get frustrated with each other. You are in a loving and committed relationship. All the same, knowing that there will be obstacles can help you make decisions ahead of time.

This chapter looks at some of the ways we may address conflict and also discusses the safety of having boundaries in our marriage.

Dealing with Conflicts

Inevitable Disagreements

When the waters get choppy, it can be easy to jump ship or avoid confrontation. Instead of getting defensive or avoiding your partner for the day, explore what it's like to let down your pride

> When the waters get choppy, it can be easy to jump ship or avoid confrontation.

and have a conversation. The knee-jerk reaction is to put a wall up. This can be a hard habit to break, but it's worth trying.

Use this Process in your Disagreements

1. **Agree on a time.** Approach your partner with the desired topic, and how soon you would like to talk about it. For example, you might say, "I'd like to talk about the dinner we had with your parents. Can we talk about it now?"

   Give your partner the option to specify another reasonable time. When you're both prepared for the conversation, both of you will likely feel safer.

2. **Check your body language.** Body language is crucial in arguments as in normal conversations. Having healthy and non-threatening body language will de-escalate the situation, so you can focus on a solution. Here are ways your body language can contribute.

   - Sit down in a relaxed position facing each other.
   - Keep arms and legs uncrossed.
   - Make eye contact.
   - Lower the pitch of your voice and speak calmly.

3. **Speak for yourself.** Instead of using "you-statements," use "I-statements." For example, instead of saying, "You completely ignored me at dinner," which suggests the implication of a pointing finger, you should rephrase the statement as "I felt disrespected at dinner because I felt ignored by you."

4. **Stay Focused.** Focus on the situation at hand instead of rehearsing situations that occurred in the past. Perhaps your spouse has a relationship with their in-laws that frustrates you. Instead of bringing

up past behaviors you did not like, refer only to the occurrence that led to this conversation.

5. Think of yourself, your partner, and your relationship separately. When you face indecision, ask yourself three questions:

- What is best for you?
- What is best for your partner?
- What is best for your relationship?

> Discussing disagreements doesn't always mean that they'll end in agreement. However, these conversations do invite compromise and understanding.

By taking the time to plan ahead, you'll both show up to the difficult conversation ready, loving, and willing to talk things out. Discussing disagreements doesn't always mean that they'll end in agreement. However, these conversations do invite compromise and understanding. They will even help you each get to know each other better.

Remain Respectful

Arguing with intention creates an environment where it's safe to disagree and make mistakes. Saying something rude at dinner doesn't have to result in a three-month silent treatment. Instead, you can have an honest conversation about it that will help you and your partner grow in deeper understanding of each other.

If your partner does something that infuriates you, do your best to address the issue in private. Insulting your spouse in front of a group of friends or strangers could be more harmful than the issue itself. It could be embarrassing for you and your partner, and can lead to a greater distance between the two of you until you can talk it out.

Give your significant other the benefit of the doubt. You know your partner. You know that they love and appreciate you. Perhaps they've had a bad day, or you had a misunderstanding. Do your best to remember that your partner is a good person and is on your team.

> While arguing isn't fun or easy, doing it in a constructive way increases intimacy in a relationship.

When you approach disagreements with this in mind, you'll feel more inspired to work as a team toward a solution. While arguing isn't fun or easy, doing it in a constructive way increases intimacy in a relationship.

Let's see what we can learn from the experience of Joe and Mary.

Case Study: Skirting the Issue

We met Joe and Mary in their early stages of marriage as they were struggling with handling disagreements. Mary was quick to jump ship during times of disagreement or whenever the couple engaged in arguments. Mary would immediately withdraw emotionally and physically while Joe was the in-your-face, let's-settle-this-now kind of communicator. While Joe wanted to get the disagreements settled, Mary wanted to retreat and deal with the issues at hand when things calmed down. The two different approaches were not working for the couple.

What we discovered was that Mary's avoidance of the resolutions of the issues was becoming problematic in the marriage, given their communication and the timeframes by which their issues were resolved. Joe described a time when he and Mary had disagreed about paying her portion of the bills and he wanted to discuss the bills in general to create a plan for having the bills paid on time. Mary immediately became defensive because she felt as an adult she didn't need to speak with him regarding the bills as she could handle that on her own. She avoided discussing the bills with Joe for several days by coming home and involving herself in either household chores that she rarely completed or hanging out with co-workers after work and coming home late.

Joe became increasingly frustrated concerning Mary's lack of concern in regards to agreeing to a time to discuss these issues and her lack of focus regarding the situation at hand. However, he decided to let the situation go. Several days later he retrieved a late notice in the mail from a company notifying them that the bill hadn't been paid. This had been Mary's pattern of avoiding issues until something major happened where confrontation was inevitable.

When Mary came home from work, Joe was waiting for her arrival to discuss the missed payment, her avoidance of developing a plan and her lack of engaging him in meaningful discussions. Joe had written out an outline of what he wanted to discuss to keep him focused on only the issues at hand, to help him remain respectful and to keep the conversation limited to relevant discussion points.

As Joe showed Mary the missed payment notice from the company, Mary refused to sit with him in the living room to discuss this and she immediately rushed to the bedroom to avoid him. Joe followed her. Mary immediately left the bedroom when Joe arrived and went back to the living room to avoid him. He followed her to the living room trying his hardest to resolve this issue, but Mary refused to discuss it. Mary retreated to the basement to watch television. Joe followed her to the basement as well, but Mary simply stared at the television. Joe asked if another time later would work, but Mary never agreed on another time to discuss this, so Joe left her alone in the basement, hoping that a little time and space would bring Mary to the point of discussion. Time and space only made Joe more frustrated and gave Mary more time to figure out how to avoid Joe and the situation.

After being alone for 15 minutes in the basement, Mary decided to leave the house. Without giving any details to Joe, Mary walked out of their home, got into her car and drove around for approximately 3 hours. She went to her city's downtown, did some shopping, stopped to get some food, walked around a little bit and then drove around some more. She then drove to the one place she knew she would get empathy, a supportive ear and someone to be on her side – her mom's house. As Mary rang the doorbell, her mom knew something was wrong because Mary seldom popped up at her home.

Mary described her side of the situation to her mom. Her mom, a divorced woman for about fifteen years, knew better. Her mom explained to her that she couldn't walk out on her marriage when disagreements occurred. Mary's mom explained that this was exactly what Mary's dad would do when they were married. Her dad would leave the home whenever there were disagreements, drive around for hours, come home and avoid resolving the issues for long periods of time. As he continued this pattern of behavior, things got progressively worse. He would not only drive for hours but he started going to bars and have a couple of drinks and then come back home smelling like alcohol. After a while, he would smell like alcohol and women. He kept leaving until at one point he never returned – and that's how they ended up divorcing.

As Mary's mom was describing these episodes, Mary remembered an incident with her older, married sister when Mary was ten years old. Mary was awakened at 2 a.m. to loud bangs on the door and heard her mother talking to her older sister. When Mary went into the living room, she saw her older sister with her one-year old daughter and a suitcase. Mary remembered that her sister had just been married for a little over one year. Her sister had packed her clothes and the baby's clothes and wanted to come back home due to the disagreements in their marriage. Her sister had started out by leaving the marital home periodically throughout that year and had finally come to the point where she wanted to permanently leave.

Mary's mom eventually talked her into going back home, working through their disagreements and engaging her husband in meaningful discussion that would resolve the conflict. Her mom confirmed to Mary that the situation with her sister was real, and highlighted learned patterns of behavior that were prevalent in the family dynamics.

After we started working with Mary, she was able to recognize her destructive patterns of avoidance and her lack of engaging in solutions to resolve conflict and disagreements. Mary apologized to Joe for her behavior during the first years of their marriage and committed to staying engaged in the struggles that had come into the marriage, assuring him that she wouldn't leave him ever again during times of disagreement.

Joe and Mary are on track with resolving issues and Joe has even become a lot less confrontational and demanding in his efforts to get the issues resolved immediately. The days of being mad for weeks without discussing the issues at hand are long gone, and they have figured out the ability to discuss issues in the marriage in a reasonable way that has them moving on quicker to resolving the issues.

Discussion

If you were Joe, how might a change in the way you handled the initial disagreements have helped the situation?

Perhaps Joe might have reviewed his tactics for getting Mary's attention which were obviously not working and getting him frustrated. This is not to excuse her behavior or to blame Joe for being confrontational. No, it had to be said there and then, especially if you were faced with your electricity being cut off.

But there may also have been opportunities to discuss her shortcomings as well as his in a less heated atmosphere. That way she would have been more likely to open up. Obviously, since she had a habit of avoidance, something deeper was going on in her psyche and he needed to let her feel comfortable about talking about it.

Putting yourself in Mary's shoes, imagine the chain of events that could have happened if your mom had taken your side and felt that it was all Joe's fault?

In Mary's case, she expected her mom to mollycoddle her, no matter what. It would have been wonderful to have a shoulder to cry on and all her creature comforts taken care of. But Mary's mother wised up to these tactics. She had seen this pattern of behavior too many times. So the straight talk helped. When it was done in a loving way, it made Mary sit up and think, helping her to remember a similar episode with her sister. It was good that her mother laid it all out before her and made her see the pattern of her father's destructive behavior and how she, too, was setting herself up for a fall. Unconditional love sometimes is tough love, love that exposes scars and causes immediate pain for the sake of growth.

> Unconditional love sometimes is tough love, love that exposes scars and causes immediate pain for the sake of growth.

This discussion leads me to talk about something that we all need to establish early in our marriage – and that is Boundaries.

Boundaries

Your yard has a fence to give you protection from unwanted visitors. It makes you feel safe. In the same way, boundaries in a marriage are meant to give you protection to guard both of you against unnecessary pain. A boundary is that line or limit which a couple sets to protect their marriage, and prevent them from hurting and manipulating one another. That line between you and your spouse separates the one from the other's dysfunctions and allocates ownership and accountability between the two.

Of course, boundaries can never form the basis of a love relationship but they do provide you with a safety net to filter out thoughtless or selfish behavior that may inadvertently hurt your partner.

> Boundaries in a marriage are meant to give you protection to guard both of you against unnecessary pain.

You and your mate should sit down and work out some ground rules of behavior to see how you can protect the atmosphere over your home. But here are some common boundaries in any marriage – and you can add your specifics later.

Faithfulness

It goes without saying that marital faithfulness is the core of your relationship. This is more than ceasing to have sexual intimacy with any other. It will also include cutting off all soul ties with former lovers – even stopping those long phone conversations, no matter how innocent. Your wife or husband is now your lover, best friend and confidante.

> It goes without saying that marital faithfulness is the core of your relationship.

"Oh, but it's between me and the woman. As long as my wife does not know, there's no harm done." Don't deceive yourself; it's not that simple:

Do you not know that he who unites himself with a prostitute is one with her in body? For it is said, "The two will become one flesh" (1 Corinthians 6:16).

When you have sexual relations or ungodly soul ties with another, you become one flesh. You (and your spouse indirectly) become partakers of all that person's multiple sex adventures and all their related dysfunctions.

Faithfulness also includes blocking off all fantasy sex partners by watching pornography or frequenting places where casual sex is easily available. Do not put yourself in places which entice you to sin. Remember what happened to the young man in Proverbs 5.

Responsibilities

Financial responsibilities have to be ironed out regarding the sharing of expenses, including the mortgage, the car, the children's education and so on. The traditional role of the husband as sole breadwinner and the wife as homemaker has become blurred, so the burden of allocating responsibilities is now on the couple. Responsibility for household chores, the children's practical needs such as transport to school and homework need to be planned, especially if both parties have full-time careers.

Respect

This is based on your high esteem for your partner and by right does not need to be protected by boundaries. But here are some of them, regardless.

- Definitely no shouting or barking at your mate
- No calling each other names apart from affectionate nicknames
- Full attention and eye contact when your mate is speaking to you
- No insulting their family or friends with rude personal remarks
- No sulking in a corner for days when you are offended
- No bringing up past offenses in an argument
- No exposing your partner's private details in front of others, even joking about her cooking and his snoring.

Confidences

What your mate has confided in you is sacred and, by disclosing it to another, you have broken trust.

Do not share confidences between you and your spouse with others whether in private or in public. What your mate has confided in you is sacred and, by disclosing it to another, you have broken trust. They may not know what you have done, but your integrity has been broken.

Space

Respect your spouse's personal property especially their laptop and mobile phone. Never look at their private emails or text messages without their permission. For that matter, do not eavesdrop on their conversations with others – on the phone or in person – pretending you are not there when you are sneaking in. These space issues become a mute point when there is infidelity involved or situations that pose an imminent danger to someone's safety. Allow your mate a place and a time to be alone to rest or do their own thing. Allowing each other space shows them that there is trust. However, do not abuse the space as an opportunity to become vulnerable or to be secretive. Remove any secrets present in the relationship, especially on your devices, that would bring harm, danger to your mate or infidelity to your relationship. If your spouse requests to view emails, text messages, apps, laptops or any other devices, you should be more than willing to allow them to see the requested information without being defensive. This is extremely important in instances when trust has been violated.

Safety

Strictly refrain from any form of physical, psychological or emotional violence. Cease from any form of emotional blackmail such as threatening to leave if an argument does not work in your favor. See that your house is safe from intruders or uninvited visitors.

Chapter 9

♥

CATCH LIFE'S CURVEBALLS

There will always be curveballs and confusion. Such is the nature of life and being in a relationship is no exception. When your partner is going through a hard time, it can be difficult to know just what to do.

In order to better understand your partner and what they need, start by listening.

Emotional/Mental Health

Emotional and mental health issues affects booming numbers of the population. These obstacles can be debilitating and scary. It's difficult to know what to say to someone who's suffering from depression, anxiety, PTSD, bipolar disorder, or any other mental health issue.

> When your spouse is hurting, it can be hard to let go of control. There's no switch you or your partner can flip to make things better.

When your spouse is hurting, it can be hard to let go of control. There's no switch you or your partner can flip to make things better. There's not a magic button that cures anxiety or a magic wand strong enough to wipe away trauma. Though this is unfortunate, it doesn't mean that the future is bleak. There is always healing power available in God Almighty.

> Because you cannot control your spouse's mental health patterns, you have a special opportunity to be a beacon of hope while your partner goes through a difficult time.

Because you cannot control your spouse's emotional or mental health patterns, you have a special opportunity to be a beacon of hope while your partner goes through a difficult time. Sometimes that just means sitting in silence, and sometimes it means talking all night long.

Ideas to Help a Partner in Distress

Listen. Give your partner the floor. Whatever they need to say, let them say it. Some emotional or mental health issues can be triggered by shame or transition. Let your partner talk their way to the root of the issue, even if you think you know better than they do.

- **Be patient**. You might find yourself having the same encouraging conversation multiple times. Perhaps you're reminding your spouse how loved they are, and they don't believe you. It can get frustrating to continuously repeat these conversations. However, your partner might need to hear it.

- **Support – don't problem solve**. Even though you want to, you cannot save or fix your partner. Instead, you can help them get professional help and be supportive and encouraging along the way. Remember, you're not solely responsible for the emotional and mental health of your spouse.

- **Take care of yourself**. Though you may not struggle with mental illness, you may still be personally affected by it through your partner. Talking about this together with a professional will make you stronger as an individual and a couple.

- **Get curious.** Do research about your partner's struggles. Their experience is unique to them, so do most of your learning from them. However, there's a lot you can learn about emotional and mental health by reading credible sources or talking to licensed professionals.

You have an opportunity to love your partner well by providing consistency and support in times of uncertainty and doubt.

Dealing with Uncertainty

Maybe your partner is currently facing a period of instability as a result of the loss of a loved one, a change of career, a mid-life crisis, or another obstacle. Regardless of the catalyst, the ground is uneven, and you have to step in as a source of guidance and support.

> While you get to be your partner's number one supporter, you are not their savior.

You play a major role in the support network of your spouse, as your spouse does for you. However, while you get to be your partner's number one supporter, you are not their savior. It's not easy to see the people we love in pain. These painful moments, however, are often huge growth milestones.

These milestones can lead to positive next steps when they're nurtured with care and attention. For example, if your spouse is grieving the loss of a childhood friend, you can provide a shoulder to cry on and a listening ear. You don't need to change the way your partner feels by distracting or avoiding the pain. But you can help your significant other cope with and feel all the necessary emotions in order to get through and beyond the difficulty. Helping your partner do something does not mean doing it for them. You can provide guidance and encouragement, while they do their own work towards personal growth.

There will always be hurdles and confusion. The beautiful thing about a loving relationship is its ability to provide a consistent strand of hope through all the inconsistencies of life.

Case Study: A Guilty Secret

I was contacted by Justin due to his casual, infrequent viewing of pornographic videos. Justin came to me in confidence as he had been married for ten years at the time. He was a public figure in his community, a leader at his church and a wonderful family man. Justin's wife had recently discovered his pornographic material on their personal computer. Justin and Jane were a happily married couple at the time that I began to coach Justin.

Justin had first engaged in pornographic magazines at the age of nine. One day his father asked Justin to look under his bed and bring his slippers. As young Justin reached under the bed, he pulled out a magazine that had a naked woman on the cover of the magazine. Being a curious child, Justin opened a few pages and saw many more beautiful women with no clothes on and became more intrigued with the magazine. Justin rolled up the magazine, tucked it inside his belt and under his shirt, and delivered the slippers to his father. Justin then took the magazine to the bathroom, locked the door and spent the next 30 minutes perusing every picture of naked women in the magazine.

From age nine until eighteen, Justin would steal his father's adult magazines and fantasize being intimate with the women on the pages. During high school and college, Justin struggled with finding the right "type" of woman that matched his physical attraction which was based solely on the images he saw in the magazines. In his senior year of college, Justin finally found the woman of his imaginary dreams. Jane was "Miss College" of the school; she was "Homecoming Queen" and an aspiring model. She was the picture of beauty that Justin had always desired based upon the images he saw throughout the years.

Justin and Jane were married immediately after college. By this time Justin had graduated from pornographic magazines to online pornographic videos. Justin managed to hide this from Jane because he was able to access the videos from his phone and would only watch them on the personal computer when no one was home. In the second year of their marriage, Jane stumbled upon some disturbing images of other women on their personal computer and asked Justin about them. He passed it off as something that may have been mistakenly downloaded but nothing to worry about as he immediately deleted them. Jane was very patient with Justin as she wanted to believe him. She had encouraging conversations with him and reminded him that she wanted to be his source of physical and emotional pleasure.

Although Jane did not know the depth of Justin's deception and addiction, she was supportive of Justin and made sure he knew that she was there if he ever needed to talk things through. Jane did not have a good feeling about the situation but wanted to allow Justin the opportunity to open up to her and reveal what emotional state his was in. Justin did not open up and left Jane in the dark.

Justin went deeper into the pornographic viewing, although he would only engage in the videos during times of emotional stress, when he and Jane were not intimate, when he was feeling the pressures of life and being married, and when he did not take care of his mental and emotional health. There were cycles of discovery by Jane throughout their marriage, but Justin was gifted at disguising the behavior, explaining the material away and masking his true struggles with pornography.

In their tenth year of marriage, Jane was required by her employer to work from home, which required downloading software that the company provided. Jane worked for a criminal justice organization that was involved in investigating cybercrimes. Jane did not realize that she had signed a waiver to allow a company approved software to scan the computer for any illegal or potentially damaging moral material on the computer being used for company business. After the scan was complete, Jane was asked to meet with her superior regarding the contents of her computer. At this meeting, her superiors showed Jane hundreds of pornographic videos that had been accessed over the last ten years of their marriage. Jane immediately broke down in tears; she was furious and completely devastated. Although Jane was aware of Justin's emotional distresses, she never could image that he would betray her in this way.

Justin and Jane stayed up all night long discussing the pornographic videos and how Justin had ended up at that point. Jane was able to gain some perspective about his situation, but she was still struggling with the uncertainty of their future and marriage. I was able to encourage Jane to be a source of guidance and support as I worked with Justin to recover from his years of pornography usage. Jane decided to be an instrumental piece to Justin's much needed network of support that he was going to need over the years. I communicated to Jane that she couldn't save Justin from this behavior and reminded her that he must put in the work to overcome these issues and behaviors.

Justin agreed to have weekly accountability with me, and he allowed me to ask hard questions regarding his viewing of pornography, his activity online and his activity with any outside influences that could affect his marriage. Justin agreed to download and pay for an accountability software, Covenant Eyes, which monitors an unlimited number of devices for any inappropriate offline and online viewing. Covenant Eyes also sends reports, that can't be manipulated by the person being monitored, directly to individuals that are identified as accountability partners. Jane, his Pastor, his best friend and I, were identified as accountability partners for Justin.

Because Jane was helpful with assisting Justin with navigating his emotional roller coasters, Justin was very successful in dealing with his pornography struggles. Jane always remained hopeful that this situation would be put behind them and that they would rejoice in the solid marriage that would result. Jane guided Justin towards getting the help he desperately needed, while allowing him to do his own work towards his personal growth and development. Justin and Jane learned that life sometimes throws us curveballs but, being a consistent strand of hope, patience and love can lead to a wonderful and productive marriage.

Discussion

Have you ever felt you've been thrown a curved ball because of your partner's emotional or mental health issues or addictions? How could you benefit from the teaching in this chapter?

> Being a consistent strand of hope, patience and love can lead to a wonderful and productive marriage.

Chapter 10

♥

UNCONDITIONAL LOVE
AND CODEPENDENCY

"Actual love, as in unconditional love, doesn't mean you
love everything about the person. It means you don't need
them to be different than they are for you to be happy."

-UNKNOWN

The last chapter highlighted our role in helping our spouse through a critical time. That is a magnanimous and heroic act. But does it mean being constantly at their beck and call? This leads me to talk about unconditional love and its various interpretations. Does unconditional love mean losing your independence? Or does it mean setting the parameters of that love? Again, what can we learn from God's unconditional love for us?

You see, unconditional love and codependency are often confused for each other. While they look fairly similar, their motivations and patterns are vastly different. Unconditional love speaks of unfailing love through all of life's circumstances, but "codependency" is "excessive emotional or psychological reliance on a partner, typically one who requires support" (Webster, 2020).

So when does unconditional love lead to codependency?

Let's first look at the concept of unconditional love and then codependency, especially in marriage.

Unconditional Love

> The only way love can last a lifetime is if it's unconditional.
> The truth is this: love is not determined by the one being
> loved but rather by the one choosing to love."
> — Stephen Kendrick, The Love Dare

> The only way love can last a lifetime is if it's unconditional. The truth is this: love is not determined by the one being loved but rather by the one choosing to love."
> – Stephen Kendrick, The Love Dare

Unconditional love implies mutual giving, openness, carrying one another's burdens, while being exposed to one another's flaws without fear or shame. At its best, unconditional love gives both partners as deep sense of security because each has emotionally bared their innermost selves to the other and yet does not feel threatened. There is no better recipe for healthy growth in a marriage in the midst of life's uncertainties.

When is unconditional love healthy?

When the couple work together to build the relationship, when the giving is reciprocal and when they help one another grow. When a couple ride out the storms of life together and make sacrifices for one another, it can only build character, resilience, and the ability to lean on one another without shame or resentment. This is a very mature form of love because it is two-way. But it has to be developed intentionally rather than left to

> When a couple ride out the storms of life together and make sacrifices for one another, it can only build character, resilience, and the ability to lean on one another without shame or resentment.

chance. One reason why it works is that boundaries have to be built into the relationship, that is, limits on behavior have to be set and the couple must be conscious of their roles and responsibilities.

When there are no proper boundaries, one partner will always seem to be doing all the giving while the other takes. In addition, false expectations may be placed on the relationship, resulting in disappointment and frustration.

What about God's unconditional love?

God's agape love is unconditional. He has loved us with an everlasting love; He has drawn us with unfailing kindness. (Jeremiah 31:3). He is faithful even when we are unfaithful. Yet, God also sets boundaries. He sets these boundaries to rein in all our excesses. He is lavish with us but it doesn't mean that He allows us to take advantage of this like pampered kids.

What do these boundaries look like? We have already seen how Jesus pictured our relationship with Him as the vine and the branches. In this passage He introduces His Father as the gardener who tends to the vine. We the branches depend on the vine to be fruitful; but look what happens to the branches that are not fruitful:

> "I am the true vine, and my Father is the gardener. He cuts off every branch in me that bears no fruit, while every branch that does bear fruit he prunes so that it will be even more fruitful. You are already clean because of the word I have spoken to you. Remain in me, as I also remain in you. No branch can bear fruit by itself; it must remain in the vine. Neither can you bear fruit unless you remain in me.

If you do not remain in me, you are like a branch that is thrown away and withers; such branches are picked up, thrown into the fire and burned" (John 1-4, 6, emphasis added).

So God gets rid of our unproductive and dysfunctional behavior so that we can be fruitful. He cuts it off. In other words, He chastises us and that period of chastisement can be painful.

The author of Hebrews wrote,

> *My son, do not regard lightly the discipline of the Lord, nor be weary when reproved by him. For the Lord disciplines the one he loves, and chastises every son whom he receives* (Hebrews 12:5-6).
>
> *...the moment all discipline seems painful rather than pleasant, but later it yields the peaceful fruit of righteousness to those who have been trained by it* (Hebrews 12:11).

> Because He loves us and wants to see us develop into strong individuals, God practices "tough" love.

Because He loves us and wants to see us develop into strong individuals, God practices "tough" love. He never gives in to our childish demands and always brings us back to His instruction manual – the Bible.

> Tough love loves unconditionally but always sets boundaries so we bear the consequences of our foolishness.

My son, do not forget my teaching, but keep my commands in your heart, for they will prolong your life many years and bring your prosperity (Proverbs 3:12).

Tough love loves unconditionally but always sets boundaries so we bear the consequences of our foolishness. When unconditional love does not set boundaries of behavior, it is easily manipulated and abused. Very often it leads to codependency where the person giving the love is severely compromised.

Let's now look at the characteristics of codependency.

Codependency

> A codependent person is one who has let another person's behavior affect him or her and who is obsessed with controlling that person's behavior.
>
> – Melody Beattie (2013), *Codependent No More*

Codependency is a way of relating to another that results in excessive care-taking and people-pleasing. Someone who is codependent typically has good intentions in sacrificing their needs for others, but this sense of responsibility for their partner's emotions and behaviors ends up becoming toxic.

In what ways is codependency expressed? Here are some ways a codependent person expresses themselves compared with a healthy person.

Codependent	Healthy
Internalizing your partner's feelings and emotions and allowing them to control your own	Being able to separate your own feelings and emotions from your partner's even though it is difficult at times
Making your partner's needs, more important than your own	Listening and empathizing but separating their emotions from yours
Ignoring or even repressing your own emotions and needs	Respecting your own emotional needs
Trying to reshape your image into how your partner wants you to be	Being comfortable as your own authentic self

Accepting your partner's negative behavior because "they are just upset."	This happens occasionally but you need to draw a clear line when it comes to dumping
Ignoring your family, friends, hobbies to take care of your partner	Having your own space to develop your own interests and friends
Trying to control or manage your partner's emotions	Detaching yourself from their unstable emotions
Trying to problem-solve for your partner when they are capable of doing it themselves	Encouraging them to be more independent
Seeing yourself as the victim of circumstances.	Seeing yourself as strong and resilient in spite of the circumstances.

Table 1: Codependent vs. Healthy Personality

We see from the Table above that the codependent person is utterly tied to their partner to the point that they have almost lost their identity and distinctiveness. On one hand, they try to manage or control the partner but, on the other, the effort of taking care of the partner weighs on them and they often see themselves as a victim of circumstances. Compare this profile with that of the healthy personality and you see a person who is loving and empathetic but who is able to draw a line between their own needs and the unreasonable demands of the other. They maintain their authentic selves while growing up to be strong and resilient.

What are the root causes of codependency?

It is true that many a time a relationship is unbalanced with one person giving more and the other person taking more than what is fair or reasonable. This could be due to a temporary setback such as an illness, addiction or financial instability. But this challenge is being worked through. There could be a degree of codependency but the caregiver is not wedded to this position and does not make it a lifelong habit.

On the other hand, real codependence goes beyond the exceptional circumstances in the desire to enable a helpless person all the time, regardless of the personal sacrifice. Many psychotherapists believe that this desire stems from a deeply rooted compulsion on the part of the caregiver to control another for the sake of their own fulfillment and completion.

Let's imagine, for instance, that a nurse in a hospice is devoted to the needs of her patient and spends hours by his bedside. The patient dies and she is grieved, which is a natural and understandable emotion. But her loss is deeper because she experiences a vacuum in her life. She then goes on to transfer her emotions to another patient as if to validate her self-worthiness. The patient also dies and the cycle goes on and on. You can see that the problem is within her.

This appears to be an innate condition born out of sometimes extremely dysfunctional families or systems. The painful traumas of our childhood and relationships throughout our lives could make us want to crave to be needed by another. We therefore attempt to use our spouses, friends, or children, as props to assure our well being, and as a way of trying to restore the emotional losses from our past. This is unhealthy and this is where therapy is needed.

Many people experience codependent tendencies at one time or another, but for those who find it to be a recurring, painful theme in their lives, you might want to ask yourself the following questions:

1. Does your sense of purpose involve making extreme sacrifices to satisfy your partner's needs?
2. Is it difficult to say no when your partner makes demands on your time and energy?
3. Do you find yourself covering your partner's problems with drugs, alcohol, or the law?
4. Do you feel trapped in your relationship, physically or emotionally?
5. Do you keep silent to avoid arguments?

We will continue the list with deeper questions about yourself.

6. Do you constantly worry about what others think of you?
7. Do you feel guilty when asserting yourself. Codependent people feel that they aren't worthy, so they feel bad about making their own needs known.
8. Do you crave approval and recognition? We all like to be noticed and appreciated. However, the codependent person takes this to an entirely different level. Many of their decisions are based on the perceived opinions of others. How often do you include the opinions of others in your decision-making process?
9. Do you fear being abandoned or alone? No one likes to feel lonely, but codependent people feel worthless unless they're helping someone else. Do you feel like you have value, even when you're spending time alone?
10. Are you more dependent on your relationship than you ought to be? Do you live and die for your relationship? Is it more important to you than anything else in your life?
11. Do you come from a dysfunctional family? If you lived in a household with emotional, physical, or sexual abuse, there's a higher possibility that you are codependent.

If you see yourself agreeing with more than 3 items on the first list and more than 4 on the second list, there is a strong likelihood that you are codependent. Codependency is a serious issue that requires professional help. Be sure that you're not confusing codependency with unconditional love. Many people that are codependent believe they are loving unconditionally. Their behavior might mimic unconditional love, but the motivation behind it is very different.

If you recognize that you are codependent, seek professional help. Here is one support group that has a program of recovery from codependence: Co-Dependents Anonymous https://coda.org/newcomers/

Now let's see what codependency can do in a marriage.

Case Study: Manipulation

Bob had come to us after just marrying Sarah four months ago. In this short period of time, Sarah noticed that Bob was extremely connected to his mother's needs that he was neglecting his own needs. Bob's mom was a single mother of two boys, and she made the decision to not marry anyone when Bob and his brother were five and three years old respectively. Several men that she dated over the years had proposed to her, but she refused to marry any of them.

She poured all her emotional, financial and physical strength into Bob and his younger brother and likewise demanded their unconditional support. As the oldest, Bob was the "man of the house" and was always responding to his mother's requests to handle certain tasks around the house because she "didn't have a man" to complete those tasks.

Bob became accustomed to "saving" his mom during situations that she could have easily handled as an adult. Bob described that once his mother had called him in the house as he was playing outside at nine years old to help her carry their hamper of clothes to the laundry room which was one room over from his bedroom. Bob understood that she was fully capable of completing this task, but because of the praise she bestowed upon him, his need to feel needed by his mother and the strong desire he had to please his mother, he obliged at her every request to complete tasks that an adult was completely capable of doing.

And so Bob's mother continuously called upon Bob for the most basic requests that she could have easily completed. Sadly, Bob saw his behaviors of being a savior to his mother as necessary for his survival. As a child, Bob became focused on keeping the household running that he ignored his own emotional and social needs. Bob associated his various roles – big brother, man of the house, mechanic and whatever his mom needed him to be – with feelings of stability and control.

These requests from Bob's mother intensified as Bob entered high school and his mother became more dependent on Bob. Bob described a time in high school when he gone on his first date. Bob left his house and drove 15 minutes to pick up his date. Approximately 30 minutes into the date, his mother called and told Bob that she had dropped a glass tray from the refrigerator, the glass had broken and shattered on the kitchen floor. She stated that she needed Bob to come home immediately to help her remove the dangerous glass from the floor as she might get injured doing so. When Bob and his date arrived, his mother was relaxing on the sofa and watching television and instructed Bob to clean up the mess, take out the trash and make sure all glass is removed before he leaves. Bob spent approximately one hour completing all his mother's requests, he missed the movie that his was supposed to attend with other friends, and he upset his date. Bob was only concerned about his mother's needs and he protected her against all verbal accusations from his date regarding his mother's behavior.

Bob spent his high school years looking for his mother's validation, praise and approval that he missed out on developing valuable friendships with others. He was convinced that only his mother's opinion and valida-tion mattered.

Since Bob was unable to set boundaries with his mother and was unable to say "no" to her many requests. He did not value himself and placed her needs above his. He even declined a four-year scholarship to an Ivy League University because the location of the school was too far away to respond to his mother's requests. Although Bob felt that he was doing an honorable duty of looking after his mother's emotional and physical well-being, he was operating in self-denial by prioritizing her needs over his needs.

Because Bob went to college close to home, he was not resting well, providing self-care and sleeping well due to the around the clock requests, and sometimes demands from his mother. On one occasion Bob described that his mother had went to a grocery store and had written a bad check. She knew that she didn't have the money in her checking account to cover the check, but she wrote the check, nonetheless. The grocery store contacted her stating that if they didn't have the money within 48 hours they were contacting the police. Instead of figuring how she was going to rectify the situation she created, she called Bob to fix her problem. Bob immediately contacted a temporary work agency for work to cover his mother's grocery bills and he used portions of his college refund to pay for the bounced check.

His behavior prevented his mother from becoming independent and learning from her own mistakes.

After his graduation from college and becoming financially stable, Bob's mother demanded that he become her caretaker by handling her finances and household chores. During this time, Bob married Sarah and the requests from his mother intensified immensely. Not only did his mother demand that Bob be her caretaker, when she was mentally and physically capable of doing it herself, she required that he do everything her way. Bob was not willing to put his foot down and set boundaries with his mother. Additionally, Bob's life was revolving around his mother. This took up his time and energy and affected his personal time with his new wife.

Although Bob was resentful towards his mother, he began to direct his anger towards Sarah. As a result of the resentment and time commitments to care for his mother, Bob's marriage was suffering from isolation, a lack of intimacy with his wife feeling abandoned and neglected. Sarah felt the strain on their marriage, their finances, their social life and their quality time. After a few short months of marriage, Sarah was ready to file for divorce because she recognized that Bob was unable to make the necessary changes to set boundaries in regards to responding to his mother's never-ending requests and demands,

By now Bob and Sarah had been married for several years. I worked with Bob for several months to set appropriate boundaries with his mother and to effectively communicate to her the importance of his needs. Bob and I worked on eliminating one responsibility at a time back to his adult mother who was capable of handling these on her own. We started with removing Bob as her caretaker – no longer taking care of her finances and her household chores – and allowing her to handle these responsibilities and face any consequences on her own.

Through all these carefully worked out measures, Bob, with Sarah's help, was able to stay the course of relinquishing the caretaker roles and not intervening when things were not successful. After much coaching and direction, Bob was able to focus on his needs so that he could properly focus on the needs of Sarah.

Think About It

In the above case study, of course we blame the mother for raising up her two sons in such a dysfunctional way. She was demanding, petty and selfish.

But let's visit the case again.

Knowing the back-story, what could Bob have done to prepare his mother and wife to face the challenges before they surfaced?

From her prior experience of the mother, what could Sarah have done to set up boundaries within the marriage "to catch the little foxes"?

How could pre-marital counseling have helped the couple have a clear understanding of the challenges ahead and a better sense of direction?

This leads us to the final question: How can wholehearted love be offered in a marriage?

First, **be realistic** in your expectations for both of you. Recognize the limitations in yourself and your spouse and don't try to set standards that put a strain on you. Be comfortable and spontaneous with each other. It isn't necessary for someone to be perfect in your eyes for you to love them unconditionally. It also isn't likely that you'll be able to change anyone either. Loving someone unconditionally means overlooking, or even appreciating, those parts of their personality and behavior that aren't what you would consider perfect. A huge part of unconditional love is accepting your partner as they are, with all their imperfections. It's far too

Wholehearted LOVE

> Loving someone unconditionally means overlooking, or even appreciating, those parts of their personality and behavior that aren't what you would consider perfect.

complicated and challenging to change someone to even seriously consider it. It's hard enough trying to change oneself!

A forgiving heart goes a long way towards reconciliation where there has been a rift or misunderstanding. Love and forgiveness go hand in hand. Practice being more forgiving in all aspects of your marriage, and forgive your partner for their shortcomings and mistakes. Don't forget to forgive yourself for all the times you messed up.

Focus on your shared vision for the future. This creates the idea of you and your partner building something as your legacy. It's the dream that you share. You can't help but feel close when you're working toward the same thing.

Based upon the many challenges we have overcome in our marriage, we know what unconditional love looks like and we want you to experience victory in your relationship as well. Remember that, in order to receive unconditional love, you must be willing and able to give it.

> A forgiving heart goes a long way towards reconciliation where there has been a rift or misunderstanding.

105

Chapter 11

CONCLUSION

Enjoy your relationship to its fullest by embracing the healthy heart habits we discussed, operating in unconditional love, and implementing the principles we've outlined in your relationships. A secure relationship allows room for growth. It gives you and your partner the space you need to reach the heights of healthy love for yourselves and for each other.

Let's recap what we've discussed:

> A secure relationship allows room for growth. It gives you and your partner the space you need to reach the heights of healthy love for yourselves and for each other.

We established the **conjugal concept** of marriage in demonstration of God's love for His church, and preparation to be His bride. Although marriage is not eternal, it is permanent on earth until death. We also saw from Ephesians 5:22-23 that the husband is the positional head over his wife to reflect the headship of Christ over His church. Finally, marriage is a union between a man and a woman and never same-sex partners.

We talked about **intimacy in marriage** and discussed the fact that intimacy provides a source of vulnerability and comfort. While sexual intimacy is important, there are other forms of intimacy that also bring about closeness and togetherness. We can have physical intimacy with our affectionate gestures; emotional intimacy by being available and support-ive; intellectual intimacy in conversations at a higher plane and share our deepest opinions and thoughts, and, finally, there is experiential intimacy in doing a lot of things together.

We learned that **disagreements are a natural part of any healthy relationship.** Instead of putting up walls and avoiding confrontation, face the disagreements and work through the obstacles in an honest and non threatening way.

Then, we discussed how life never promised to be predictable, and it certainly isn't. **Curveballs** will be thrown in your direction and your partner will need extra support and encouragement. You can provide this by listening with care and compassion. Your support is especially needed if your partner is struggling with mental health issues and, even if you cannot help them directly, you can be a source of stability. There are other situations that life throws our way. Jobs are lost, friends are grieved, and a whole set of conundrums appear every day. These struggles are a part of life. They foster growth as a couple and as individuals.

We also discussed that, like the physical heart, the **spiritual heart has four chambers:**

The Intellect, which thinks, understands, meditates and believes.

The Conscience, which can be pierced by conviction of our sins or regret for hurts we have caused. Remember that *"Godly sorrow brings repentance that leads to salvation and leaves no regret, but worldly sorrow brings death"* (2 Corinthians 7:10).

The Will, purposes, has intentions and obeys. Its intentions are known to God, for while people look at the outward appearance, the Lord looks at the heart.

The Emotions experience anguish, desires, and love as when Paul dis-closes, *"For I wrote you out of great distress and anguish of heart and with*

many tears, not to grieve you but to let you know the depth of my love for you"
(2 Corinthians 2:4).

We also discussed Heart Blockages and Uneven Rhythms.

> We can pull down these strongholds by denouncing every lie of the enemy and holding every thought and imagination captive to obedience to Christ (2 Corinthians 10:3-5).

When our hearts get blocked it's the love that gets blocked out. What blocks this true love is spiritual plaque. Some of the forms spiritual plaque can take are: bitterness, unforgiveness, resentment, trauma, betrayal, selfishness, mistrust, unbelief, willful ignorance of the bible. All these allow strongholds of resistance to God's word to form in our heart allowing Satan to infiltrate and establish his kingdom there. But we can pull down these strongholds by denouncing every lie of the enemy and holding every thought and imagination captive to obedience to Christ (2 Corinthians 10:3-5).

Again, sometimes our heartbeat is irregular and we need to examine ourselves to ask whether we are walking ahead of God's timing or are too lethargic in our assignment. Close fellowship with God especially through meditating on the word will help you get back on track. When we lay our head on Jesus' chest just like the disciple John did, we will hear His heartbeat.

So having an open heart in marriage is vitally important.

An open heart wills to trust the spouse because it trusts God. But we have to be wise and not be trusting in everything especially where we have been disappointed and betrayed. But Jesus showed that you can love despite the betrayals. Remember that Jesus knew who was about to betray

Him. Nevertheless He broke bread at Passover with them all including Judas (see 1 Corinthians 11:23-25).

And that did not stop Him from loving even His accusers all the way to the cross. He did not completely trust His bride, but He loved her and gave Himself up for her. Why is this important? Because people make mistakes; they sin; they hurt us. You don't have to trust your spouse in all things especially in areas where they have shown vulnerability like keeping money, telling the truth or sexual faithfulness – but you nevertheless love them and cover them with your prayers.

We then discussed the importance of healing for the wounded heart.

We have talked already about the wounds we suffer when the evil one has been working his lies on us. Some of our resentments are due to his wicked interpretation of the past events of our lives. But some of them are due to legitimate hurts or betrayals, sometimes by our spouse, and we need to face up to the fact.

It can be hard sometimes to be aware that you have not completely forgiven someone for hurting you. One test is whether you are triggered when the memory of that wrong surfaces. However, remember we are not asked to forget the facts – what was done cannot be undone. But the pain should over time be diminished until it is only a trace. When the pain is still as real as if it happened yesterday, chances are you haven't forgiven deeply enough – from the heart. Seek counsel or the help of a prayer partner to help you retrace those painful memories, and ask for God's grace so that you can forgive from the heart. Do not allow yourself to be tormented any longer like the unforgiving steward who could not forgive and was made subject to the torturers:

> *"This is how my heavenly Father will treat each of you unless you forgive your brother or sister from your heart"* (Matthew 18:35).

Finally, we discussed the concept of unconditional love versus codependency.

Unconditional love is God's agape love. It's a love that gives, sacrifices and seeks the highest good for another. What a joy when two people can experience and reciprocate that love! But unconditional love must come with boundaries which protect that relationship from manipulation and abuse. God, too, though He loves us unconditionally will chastise us if we step out of His boundaries (His commandments) because He wants us to grow and be fruitful. When a relationship has few boundaries, it can result in codependency, which is a toxic relationship full of manipulation and control.

> Unconditional love is God's agape love. It's a love that gives, sacrifices and seeks the highest good for another.

We have now reached the end of our journey to having a wholehearted marriage. We have discussed the heart and how, just as there are filters that keep the physical aspects healthy and provide health and vitality to the rest of the body, so are there spiritual/emotional filters that protect and arm the spiritual heart. With an open heart, a loving heart, and a heart for God and for His truth, we can now have God-glorifying, fulfilling, and rewarding Christian marriages until death do us part, or until Christ returns for His radiant Bride at the end of all days.

Before we close we want to share our thoughts from a few verses of that famous passage on love in 1 Corinthians 13:

> *Love suffers long and is kind; love does not envy; love does not parade itself, is not puffed up; does not behave rudely, does not seek its own, is not provoked, thinks no evil; does not rejoice in iniquity, but rejoices in the truth; bears all things, believes all things, hopes all things, endures all things.*
>
> *Love never fails* (1 Corinthians 13:4-8 NKJV).

This is agape love at its finest because it typifies the way God loves us. This love is not a feeling but a choice, the choice of being kind, selfless, considerate, and enduring. It does not express itself in feelings and sentiments but in ACTIONS. It is other-directed rather than inward to touch lives. It is radical in the sense that it does not depend on the one being loved, but on the commitment of the one acting in love. Because it's God's love, it is bigger than us and our limitations.

And, if God can give us such a love, then let's receive it. If we receive it by faith, He will empower us to walk in it. The following are some honest responses to the action words listed above in relation to others, particularly my spouse:

Love suffers long and is kind… endures all things (v.8): I notice that hurting people tend to lash out at others. But, even when I go through hardship, God's love in me can help me show kindness. Kindness is so close to God's heart because it is His kindness that leads us to repentance (Romans 2:4).

love does not envy: Envy reflects the nature of Satan who can't stand God's people being blessed. Because I have God's love within me, I am content with what I have and I rejoice in the success of another – I say, "If God can do it for them, He will do it for me."

love does not parade itself, is not puffed up: I do not show off my achievements or feel superior because of my abilities. I have learned to give God thanks for every good thing that comes to me, acknowledging that every good gift comes from God (James 1:17).

does not behave rudely: I display good manners, not to show that I am cultured, but to show respect for others, their culture and sensitivities. Therefore, I avoid making divisive remarks intentionally.

does not seek its own: (I am working on this one.) I will put the well-being of my spouse and the things that concern them, including their family above my own.

is not provoked: I carry very little offense because I have been forgiven and have God's grace to forgive my spouse. I have let go of past wrongs and hold no record of evil.

thinks no evil: I do not harbor evil in my heart because I am cleansed daily by the blood of Jesus (1 John 1:7).

does not rejoice in iniquity: No longer do I have a "serve-them-right" mentality" when I see others fall into sin or some misfortune. Instead, I pray for their restoration. I remember the words of Paul when he tells us, *"Brothers and sisters, if someone is caught in a sin, you who live by the Spirit should restore that person gently"* (Galatians 6:1).

rejoices in the truth: The truth of God's word is continually setting me free from bondage. It is bringing light into the dark areas of my life and my marriage.

bears all things: I am learning to cast my burdens on the Lord and less on people, though I do ask my prayer partners to pray with me. It is difficult to understand when trials come upon me but I am learning to stand on James 1:2-4: *"Consider it pure joy, my brothers and sisters, whenever you face trials of many kinds, because you know that the testing of your faith produces perseverance. Let perseverance finish its work so that you may be mature and complete, not lacking anything."*

believes all things: Without being gullible, I prefer to accept what my spouse says at face value rather than quiz them about everything. What a waste of energy!

hopes all things: Because I pray every day for my spouse, I believe in them to do good, no matter what they did in the past. I believe that the Holy Spirit is doing a good work in their life. I used to be a pessimist but now I have the calm expectation that all things will work together for good (Romans 8:28).

And, finally, "**love never fails**." When you put your marriage in the center of God's will and when you treat your partner with love and respect, you can be assured that God will bless your relationship. He will multiply what you have sown. You may be going through a very difficult time but know that He will never fail you. He will give you the desires of your heart.

What are your responses to 1 Corinthians 13? It may be a good idea to write them down for surely God is changing us from glory to glory!

One final thought. Do you know that Jesus' first miracle in the gospel of John was at the marriage feast of Cana? This is very significant to us because it highlights the miracles that God wants to do in our marriages. The wine had run out and His mother came to Him. He asked what that had to do with Him. She then instructed the servants, "Whatever He says to you, do it." So Jesus told the servants to go and fill the water pots with water. They filled the pots with water and drew the liquid out, and then served the master of the feast. He jumped up and immediately congratulated the host with, "You have saved the good wine for the last" (see John 2:1-10).

Let us pray:

> Lord, we receive this word for our marriages. We may have a young marriage fresh with hope. Or we may be in a struggling marriage full of uncertainty. Or it may be a faded marriage where the things we used to do and the passion we felt are no longer there. And yet, Lord, Your first miracle was for marriages. You had not planned for it because it was not yet Your time – but the Father orchestrated it.

So You changed the water into wine. You wanted this to be a time of celebration and for the marriage to be a happy one. You want the same for our marriage. And so You have saved the best wine for the last. We receive it, Lord. Do a miracle now, Lord, and let the wine of our first love come back to life – only better. Thank You, Father, in Jesus' name we pray.

WEEKEND of Love

We invite you and your spouse to attend the Weekend of Love Retreat where you will receive marriage-altering biblical principles that you can apply to your daily lives and make your marriage stronger. In many of our sessions you will learn how to:

- Receive your spouse as a gift.
- Clarify roles as husbands and wives.
- Resolve conflict in the marriage relationship.
- Maintain a vital intimate connection.
- Express forgiveness to one another.
- Create an even deeper level of communication & intimacy.

Our speakers will show you exactly how to pursue a marriage that really works through stories of their own breakthroughs and blunders. We want you to leave the weekend with encouragement, hope and practical tools to build and grow your relationship.

For more details and to register for our upcoming retreats, visit our website at **www.weekendoflove.online**. If you have questions regarding our upcoming retreats, send us an email at **info@weekendoflove.online**.

CPSIA information can be obtained
at www.ICGtesting.com
Printed in the USA
JSHW010156170423
40345JS00003B/11